# Cambridge First Certificate

# Examination Practice 5

*University of Cambridge*
*Local Examinations Syndicate*

**CAMBRIDGE**
UNIVERSITY PRESS

Published by the Press Syndicate of the University of Cambridge
The Pitt Building, Trumpington Street, Cambridge CB2 1RP
40 West 20th Street, New York, NY 10011–4211, USA
10 Stamford Road, Oakleigh, Melbourne 3166, Australia

© Cambridge University Press 1993

First published 1993

Printed in Great Britain
at the University Press, Cambridge

ISBN 0 521 44671 6  Student's Book
ISBN 0 521 44672 4  Teacher's Book
ISBN 0 521 44673 2  Set of 2 cassettes

GO

# Contents

# Acknowledgements

The authors and publishers are grateful to the following for permission to reproduce texts and illustrations. It has not been possible to identify sources of all the material used and in such cases the publishers would welcome information from copyright owners.

Jonathan Cape Ltd and Houghton Mifflin Company for the extract on pp. 4–5 from *A Journey in Ladakh* by Andrew Harvey © 1983, and Jonathan Cape Ltd and Curtis Brown for the extract on p. 85 from *Enthusiasms* by Bernard Levin; *High Life*, the inflight magazine of British Airways, for the extract on pp. 7–8 by James Wilkinson, in the February 1988 magazine; Southbank Publishing Group for the extract on p. 25 from *Practical Health*, Winter 1988; West Sussex County Library Service for the extract on pp. 26–7 from their information booklet; Chatto & Windus for the extract on pp. 41–2 from *Under the Net* and the extract on pp. 60–1 from *The Good Apprentice*, both by Iris Murdoch; Weatherhill Inc for the extract on pp. 43–4 from *The art of the Japanese kite* by Tal Streeter; Victor Gollancz Ltd for the extract on pp. 83–4 from *Don't look now* by Daphne du Maurier.

# To the student

This book is for candidates preparing for the University of Cambridge First Certificate in English examination and provides practice in all the written and oral papers. It contains 5 complete tests. The tests are based on the First Certificate examinations set in 1990 and 1991 although the listening tests, Paper 4, include some items from more recent examinations. The examination consists of 5 papers as follows:

Paper 1 Reading Comprehension (1 hour)
    *Section A* consists of 25 multiple-choice items in the form of a sentence with a blank to be filled in by 1 of 4 words or phrases.
    *Section B* consists of 15 multiple-choice items based on 3 or more reading passages of different types.

Paper 2 Composition (1½ hours)
    There are 5 topics from which you choose 2. The range of topics includes a letter, a description, a narrative, a discursive composition or a speech. There is also a topic based on optional reading. (In these books the questions based on optional reading are set on the kind of books that are prescribed each year. These are *not* the actual books prescribed for any particular year; they are just given as examples.)

Paper 3 Use of English (2 hours)
    There are exercises of various kinds which test your control of English usage and grammatical structure. There is also a directed writing exercise where you study a text often containing an illustration, map or diagram, from which you must extract the required information and present it in a coherent form.

Paper 4 Listening Comprehension (20 to 30 minutes)
    You answer a variety of questions on recorded passages (normally 4) from English broadcasts, interviews, announcements, phone messages and conversations. Each passage is heard twice.

Paper 5 Interview (about 15 minutes)
    You take part in a theme-based conversation with the examiner. Photographs, extracts from authentic materials and problem solving activities, all linked by theme, are used to stimulate the discussion. You may take Paper 5 alone or with one or two other candidates and you may, if you wish, talk about one of the optional reading texts.

# Practice Test 1

## PAPER 1   READING COMPREHENSION   (1 hour)

*Answer all questions. Indicate your choice of answer in every case* **on the separate answer sheet** *already given out, which should show your name and examination index number. Follow carefully the instructions about how to record your answers. Give* **one answer only** *to each question. Marks will not be deducted for wrong answers: your total score on this test will be the number of correct answers you give.*

### SECTION  A

*In this section you must choose the word or phrase which best completes each sentence.* **On your answer sheet** *indicate the letter A, B, C or D against the number of each item 1 to 25 for the word or phrase you choose.*

1   He refused to give up work, ................. he'd won a million pounds.
   A despite      B however      C even though      D as though

2   They were ................. for smuggling jewellery into the country.
   A judged      B arrested      C accused      D warned

3   At the end of the winter, the price of winter clothes in the shops
   usually ................. .
   A drops      B lowers      C sinks      D reduces

4   For this recipe to be successful, you ................. cook the meat for at least two
   hours in a moderate oven.
   A need      B must      C ought      D will

5   Have you got time to discuss your work now or are you ................. to leave?
   A thinking      B planned      C around      D about

6   I don't see any ................. in arriving early at the theatre if the show doesn't
   start until 9 o'clock.
   A cause      B aim      C point      D reason

7   Would you mind ................. these plates a wipe before putting them in the
   cupboard?
   A making      B doing      C getting      D giving

8  The police are looking for a man of ............... height.
   A  medium     B  extra     C  tall     D  special

9  She did all the work ............... her own.
   A  by     B  on     C  for     D  with

10  The children won't go to sleep ............... we leave a light on outside their
   bedroom.
   A  except     B  otherwise     C  unless     D  but

11  I wrote to the company ............... them for a catalogue.
   A  demanding     B  asking     C  enquiring     D  applying

12  ............... Patrick, he can't possibly go alone – he's far too young.
   A  As for     B  As if     C  As     D  As far as

13  Dinner will be ready soon. Can you please ............... the table?
   A  lay     B  settle     C  make     D  put

14  Please ............... and see us some time – you're always welcome.
   A  come to     B  come about     C  come round     D  come away

15  I was sitting in a cafe ............... afternoon when I saw the Prime Minister pass
   by.
   A  an     B  the     C  in     D  one

16  The doctor arranged for me to see the ............... at the hospital about the pain
   in my back.
   A  expert     B  specialist     C  speciality     D  expertise

17  There are ............... when I have to work very hard.
   A  times     B  at times     C  from time to time     D  a long time

18  I have to leave before seven and so ............... .
   A  leave you     B  you have     C  you do     D  do you

19  You ............... better be careful not to miss the train!
   A  would     B  should     C  had     D  did

20  Although we have a large number of students, each one receives ...............
   attention.
   A  individual     B  only     C  alone     D  single

21  By half past ten tomorrow morning I ............... along the motorway.
   A  will drive     B  am driving     C  drive     D  will be driving

22  I had to give a full ................ of my camera when I reported it stolen.
    A  account    B  detail    C  information    D  description

23  I hope you don't mind me ................ so late at night.
    A  telephoning    B  to telephone    C  telephone    D  to have
    telephoned

24  I'd be very ................ to go to Japan one day.
    A  interested    B  enjoyable    C  fond    D  hopeful

25  The bus ................ from High Street to Station Road is 60p.
    A  cost    B  fare    C  payment    D  charge

## SECTION B

*In this section you will find after each of the passages a number of questions or unfinished statements about the passage, each with four suggested answers or ways of finishing. You must choose the one which you think fits best.* **On your answer sheet, indicate the letter A, B, C or D against the number of each item 26–40 for the answer you choose. Give one answer only** *to each question. Read each passage right through before choosing your answers.*

FIRST PASSAGE

The last time I saw Ananda we talked at the top of a mountain, in his cave, on a wild spring day, looking across the plains to the sea. He lived in a cave in Kataragama, the sacred place at the heart of Sri Lanka. He said he could not leave it now that he had found he had everything he wanted. His last painting was the blue rainbow that he had painted in colours from earth and stone over the doorway to his cave.

I had walked for hours to see him, through a cloud of white butterflies. It was a month after our first meeting. His face had lost its look of sadness. He was thin and tanned. He took me into his cave, and we sat in the soft dark for a while without saying anything.

'There are snakes here, you know,' he said. 'But they do not bite if they know you are harmless. Sometimes as I sit here thinking, they come and brush past me.'

I gave him a copy of the Sonnets to Orpheus, by Rilke. He handed it back to me, gently. 'I do not read any more. You keep it.' Then he took me up to the top of the mountain, just above his cave, and we walked slowly round the small tree he had planted there.

Just before we parted, Ananda said to me, 'I had a dream about you last week. I saw you in a small room, sitting quietly. Out of the window behind you I saw mountains, snow-covered mountains. You will find that room.'

4

'I hope so.'

I must have sounded doubtful, because he said again, 'No. I am certain you will.'

'Was there anyone else in the room?'

'Yes. Several people. They were sitting with their backs to me and so I couldn't see who they were.'

'Do you have any idea where the room was?'

'No. But it was very much like a room I once stayed in at a temple near Lhasa. It was definitely a Tibetan room. There was a large painting on the wall, but it was in shadow and so I cannot tell you what its subject was. You have an inner relation with Tibet and Tibetan philosophy; you will have to explore it sooner or later!'

I walked down the hill, disbelieving and amazed at what Ananda had said. He called after me, 'Be happy! Be happy!' and I turned and saw him high on his rock, a small orange bird.

26  How did Ananda look to the writer the first time he met him?
   A thin    B unhappy    C pale    D wise

27  What do we learn of the snakes in Ananda's cave?
   A They can be dangerous.
   B They do not bite.
   C They are frightened of Ananda.
   D They make good pets.

28  Ananda dreamed of a room
   A where they had been together.
   B which he knew from a painting.
   C which neither of them knew.
   D where he had once stayed.

29  What was the writer's reaction to the description of the dream?
   A He was astonished.
   B He was afraid.
   C He was upset.
   D He was disappointed.

30  What do we learn of Ananda's life?
   A He was unable to read or write.
   B He suffered from loneliness.
   C He longed to return to Tibet.
   D He had chosen to live in this way.

SECOND PASSAGE

Consider the following facts: (1) Antisocial behaviour among the young (crime, violence etc.) is increasing, and their educational standards are falling; (2) Children are eating more so-called 'junk (or rubbish) food'. Could these two facts be connected? Until recently most expert opinion would have made fun of the question itself. Now, it seems, the experts may have to think again, taking into account the results of recently completed scientific trials, which have dramatically demonstrated the effects of children's food on their behaviour and intellectual performance.

The central issue behind the new trials concerns the importance of vitamins. For years those interested in healthy food have claimed we don't get enough goodness from modern processed food and that we all need extra vitamins and minerals to be really healthy. Established medical opinion tends to laugh at this idea, saying that for the vast majority of us a normal diet contains more than enough goodness, and that taking expensive vitamin and mineral supplements is throwing money away.

It is hardly surprising, therefore, that the new studies were carried out by people with no professional background in food whatever. Yet they may be the most important studies on children's food this decade. Gwilym Roberts was, until recently, the senior science teacher at Darland High School in North Wales. Over the past ten years he has developed an interest in food, partly because he found taking vitamin pills gave him 'more energy', but also because he began to notice disturbing changes in his pupils. 'In the last eight years or so I've found many more pupils lacking in concentration; they seem to have difficulty following the lessons in class. Similar observations have been made by teachers right across the country.' Roberts also noticed that his pupils' eating habits were changing, and felt his two observations might be connected. So he undertook to make a detailed record of what 100 of his pupils ate over a three-day period. He was shocked: 'some of them come to school with no breakfast, so in the morning they fill themselves up with crisps and sweets from the corner shop. The same thing happens at break time and lunch time.' In the past children could have been expected to receive a proper midday meal at school but, as more schools have been officially encouraged to adopt self-service systems, many children choose their own food – with obvious results.

When the diets of Roberts' pupils were analysed for their food content, they were found to be lacking in an average of ten vitamins and minerals, according to amounts officially recommended for children. Roberts' analysis, although alarming, is not particularly surprising – four other recent surveys of British children have all reported a significant lack of essential vitamins.

Could the poor diet of some of his pupils, asked Roberts, be a possible cause of their poor performance in class?

31  Up to now, any suggestion that diet and behaviour could be connected
would have been
A welcomed.    B supported.    C laughed at.    D looked into.

32  Opinion on the subject is now beginning to change thanks to
A advisers to the food industry.
B those carrying out scientific trials.
C those interested in health food.
D established medical opinion.

33  Mr Roberts
A has a professional background in food.
B is now a science teacher in North Wales.
C has benefited from taking extra vitamins.
D was a teacher of science for ten years.

34  Roberts first became interested in his pupils' diet when
A they failed to attend lessons.
B they seemed to find their lessons a waste of time.
C they began eating food during their lessons.
D they found it harder to pay attention in lessons.

35  The results of Mr Roberts' study showed that
A most pupils never had a proper meal at home.
B 100 of his pupils ate less over a three-day period.
C most pupils chose the wrong type of food to eat.
D most pupils had a proper meal at school.

36  A closer analysis of the pupils' diets showed that pupils
A had on average ten vitamins and minerals a day.
B needed an extra ten vitamins and minerals a day.
C were taking sufficient amounts of vitamins and minerals each day.
D were eating a worse diet than most other British children.

THIRD PASSAGE

It is not true that the British talk about the weather more than any other nation.
In many parts of the world the weather holds just as much fascination. Part of
the fascination arises because the weather in many parts of the world is very
difficult to forecast. Because Britain is an island sandwiched between a large
continent and a large ocean, slight changes in direction of winds in the Atlantic
or movements in areas of high or low pressure can make a major difference to
our weather.
    Most of the time our weather is unremarkable. But in the last few years

weather patterns have been causing so much trouble that it raises the question – is the weather changing to such an extent that it amounts to a change in the climate?

It's a question that is very difficult to answer. The daily and weekly variations in weather are so great that it takes years of careful measurement to detect changes in the average weather from year to year. And to detect changes in the climate involves the worldwide application of a whole number of scientific investigations.

However, looking at the distant past and estimating what may happen in the future based on theoretical possibilities, it seems there are two possibilities. The world could be slipping back towards another ice age. But in the shorter term what man is doing may well lead to a heating up of the planet which could delay, if not prevent, any forthcoming ice age.

It is sudden and unexpected weather which makes people wonder what is happening to our climate – like the once-in-a-lifetime experience of the vicious storm which swept southern England in autumn 1987. The southern states of the USA are used to such storms, the southern part of Britain isn't. And when literally millions of trees were uprooted and millions of pounds worth of damage was done to houses, farms and businesses, people wondered just what was going on. It was probably the worst storm in South-East Britain for some 300 years.

37  People are more interested in the weather in places where
   A  the weather changes often.
   B  weather forecasts may be wrong.
   C  the sea affects the climate.
   D  the wind makes a big difference.

38  It is very difficult for scientists to discover
   A  how great the weather changes are.
   B  if the weather is getting worse.
   C  if the climate is changing.
   D  what causes so many changes.

39  Scientists now think that
   A  it is impossible to say what the weather will be like.
   B  in future the weather will be the same as in the past.
   C  it will become hotter all over the world.
   D  the world will certainly be covered with ice.

40  What does the storm of 1987 show us?
   A  Storms can be very damaging to trees and property.
   B  Britain's climate is becoming more like that of the USA.
   C  We no longer know what weather to expect.
   D  The climate in South-East Britain has been getting worse for 300 years.

# PAPER 2   COMPOSITION   (1½ hours)

*Write **two only** of the following composition exercises. Your answers must follow exactly the instructions given and must be of between 120 and 180 words each.*

1   After living in a village all your life, you have moved to a city to work. Write a letter to a good friend in the village describing your new life and how you feel about the change.

2   A group of students from your school has just ended a two-week visit to a school in another country. At the farewell party, you make a speech of thanks explaining what you have enjoyed most. Write what you say.

3   You arranged a special celebration or outing for your grandmother's birthday. Describe how she spent her day.

4   'People today spend too much time and money on clothes.' What do you think?

5   Based on your reading of *one* of these books, write on **one** of the following.

   R. L. STEVENSON: *Dr Jekyll and Mr Hyde*
   One chapter of the book describes the Carew murder case. Who was the murderer and why was it impossible for the police to find him?

   MAYA ANGELOU: *I Know Why the Caged Bird Sings*
   Describe two people who were important to the author during her early life in Stamps, and explain why they were important.

   LAURIE LEE: *Cider with Rosie*
   Describe some of the social events that took place in Laurie Lee's village and the part he played in them.

# PAPER 3   USE OF ENGLISH   (2 hours)

1   *Fill each of the numbered blanks in the following passage. Use only* **one** *word in each space.*

One of the worst journeys I have ever experienced occurred a few weeks ago. I (1) .......................... booked a cheap flight to Switzerland so the ticket could not be changed (2) .......................... any way. (3) .......................... I missed the flight, I would not be (4) .......................... to use the ticket for any alternative journey.

When I reached the railway station, I was told that (5) .......................... the trains were running late; this meant I would (6) .......................... the connecting train for the airport. A loudspeaker announcement helpfully (7) .......................... us that an extra train would (8) .......................... provided, so we need not worry. Nothing could have been further from the (9) .......................... . The extra train did not arrive. I inquired (10) .......................... buses, but the last one for the airport had left! There was only one solution; I (11) .......................... to take a taxi. Dragging my suitcases behind me I hurried outside (12) .......................... found a taxi. 'It's a long way. It'll (13) .......................... you a lot,' the taxi (14) .......................... warned me. I knew that, but the taxi fare would be cheaper (15) .......................... having to buy another plane ticket.

We arrived (16) .......................... the airport with about twenty minutes (17) .......................... spare. I jumped out, looked in my bag (18) .......................... my purse and to my horror discovered it was missing! The taxi driver was pleasant but firm. My suitcases were locked in the boot and there they would stay (19) .......................... I found a way of paying (20) .......................... . Of course, I never caught my plane.

2  *Finish each of the following sentences in such a way that it means the same as the sentence printed before it.*

EXAMPLE:  I haven't enjoyed myself so much for years.

ANSWER:  It's years *since I enjoyed myself so much.*

a)  'Don't leave the house until I get back, William,' his mother said.

William's mother told ...................................................................................

b)  I'd rather not see him tomorrow.

I don't ...................................................................................

c)  Alice's strange ideas astonished everybody.

Everybody ...................................................................................

d)  It was careless of you to leave the windows open last night.

You shouldn't ...................................................................................

e)  You will catch a cold if you don't keep your feet dry.

Unless ...................................................................................

f)  It looks like rain to me.

I ...................................................................................

g)  This is the most delicious cake I have ever tasted.

I have ...................................................................................

h)  The people who were there didn't notice anything unusual.

No-one ...................................................................................

i)  She left university two years ago.

It is ...................................................................................

j)  The gate is closed to stop the children running into the road.

The gate is closed so that ...................................................................................

3  **In sentences a) – e),** *fill each of the blanks with* **one** *suitable word which refers to the group of things mentioned in that sentence.*

EXAMPLE:  I've bought carrots, onions and potatoes. Do we need any more *vegetables?*

a) The table, chairs and sofa were new but all the other
............................................. was second-hand.

b) Helen likes oranges, apples and bananas but won't eat any other kind of
............................................. .

c) Bag-snatching, car theft and burglary are some of the most common
............................................. the city police have to deal with.

d) Buses and taxis are allowed to use that street but all other
............................................. are prohibited.

e) This shop has a wide range of ............................................., such as dolls, model
cars and train sets, for children up to the age of ten.

**In sentences f) – j),** *fill each of the blanks with* **one** *suitable word which completes the expression formed from* **put.**

EXAMPLE: The government has put *up* the tax on tobacco again.

f) Mark put ............................. so much weight during the winter that none of
his summer clothes fitted any more.

g) The telephone operator couldn't put me ............................. to the Director
because he was engaged.

h) The firemen took three hours to put ............................. the fire.

i) The unexpected fall of snow meant that the football match was put
............................. for a week.

j) Oh, that terrible noise! I can't put ............................. with it any longer!

4   *Complete the numbered gaps in the following conversation.*

Lesley has recently arrived at the Smiths' house where she is going to stay
while doing a course. She and Mrs Smith are now having a chat.

Mrs Smith: I hope you'll enjoy staying with us. Is there anything you want
to ask?

Lesley:   Actually, yes, I have got a few questions about practical things.
My room looks very nice, but I didn't notice a table there and I
expect I'll have lots of work from college. Is there (1) .............................
.......................................................................................................... ?

Mrs Smith: The dining room is free all day, except from six to eight in the
evening. You can use it whenever you like.

Lesley: Fine. My next question is about dirty clothes. Where (2) ........................

..................................................................................................... ?

Mrs Smith: There's a washing machine and a drier in the kitchen. I'll show
you how to use them.

Lesley: What (3) ............................................................................................... ?

Mrs Smith: Not too early – at 7.45 am, and dinner is at 6.30 pm. I think you
said you'd be having lunch at college.

Lesley: That's right. And talking of college, how (4) ...................................

..................................................................................................... ?

Mrs Smith: There's a bus stop at the end of this road, and the bus goes
straight to the college. It'll take you about twenty minutes.

Lesley: That's not too bad. I expect I'll want to go out in the evenings.

What (5) ............................................................................................ ?

Mrs Smith: Well, there are regular buses from the centre of the town but
only until 10.30 at night.

Lesley: Just one more thing. I'm really keen on keeping fit, and someone
told me there is a sports centre in town, but you have to be a

member. Do you know how (6) ...................................................... ?

Mrs Smith: You get a form from the office and pay a membership fee of £10.
Then you pay 50 pence every time you use the facilities.

5  *You live in the pretty, historic village of Borley (population 560), 10 miles
   north-east of Laxton. The Laxton Town Council is planning to build a new
   'Leisure Centre' in the area, with a theatre, sports facilities, youth club and
   shopping mall. The aim is to provide more services for the busy people of Laxton
   without increasing the number of buildings in the crowded town itself. Laxton
   people have suggested four different places for the Centre, which are indicated on
   the map below as sites 1, 2, 3 and 4.* **Use the information given** *to help you
   complete the three paragraphs on page 15 opposite.* **Give reasons for your
   choices.**

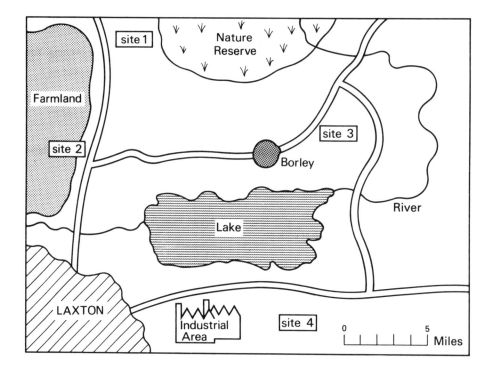

**Laxton – A Town which looks to the Future**

Some statistics:

| | |
|---|---|
| Population: | 103,000 |
| Unemployment: | 2.5% |
| Under 25s: | 38% |
| Car Owners: | 54% |
| Residents over the age of 65: | 20% |

a) The Town Council will probably choose ..........................................................................

..........................................................................................................................................

..........................................................................................................................................

..........................................................................................................................................

..........................................................................................................................................

..........................................................................................................................................

..........................................................................................................................................

b) Another possibility is ....................................................................................................

..........................................................................................................................................

..........................................................................................................................................

..........................................................................................................................................

..........................................................................................................................................

..........................................................................................................................................

..........................................................................................................................................

c) I hope they do not choose ...........................................................................................

..........................................................................................................................................

..........................................................................................................................................

..........................................................................................................................................

..........................................................................................................................................

..........................................................................................................................................

..........................................................................................................................................

# PAPER 4   LISTENING COMPREHENSION
## (about 30 minutes)

### PART ONE

*You will hear a telephone conversation about booking hotel accommodation. Look at the booking form below and complete the missing information. Some information has been filled in for you.*

---

## SKIPTON TOURIST ACCOMMODATION OFFICE
### *Hotel/Guest House Booking Form*

**GUEST**

Mr/Mrs/Ms/Miss (delete as applicable)  | 1 |

Surname:  | 2 |

Initials:  | 3 |

Address:  | 4 |

Phone:  | 5 |

**ACCOMMODATION**
Address: .......... *Hillview,* ..........................................................

| 6 |

**ACCOMMODATION BOOKED:** (tick as applicable)

| 7 | Single Room ☐          Single Room with Bath ☐

Double Room ☐          Double Room with Bath ☐

Twin Room ☐          Twin Room with Bath ☐

Cost per night: .......... *£12·50* ..........................

Number of nights:  | 8 |

Date from:  | 9 |

Deposit to pay:  | 10 | £ |

---

## PART TWO

*You will now hear a student and her landlady talking about evening classes. For questions 11–20, decide whether the statements are* TRUE *or* FALSE, *and put a tick (√) in the appropriate box.*

|  | TRUE | FALSE |
|---|---|---|
| 11 The landlady found out information about evening classes. | | |
| 12 The classes are held very near the student's house. | | |
| 13 The student is undecided about cookery classes. | | |
| 14 The student would love to go swimming. | | |
| 15 The student is no good at drawing. | | |
| 16 The landlady thinks that the student would find a computer course useful. | | |
| 17 The student found the computer course very easy. | | |
| 18 The student has practised self-defence before. | | |
| 19 Self-defence is the only course in which the student is interested. | | |
| 20 The landlady thinks that modern dancing is more suitable than self-defence. | | |

## PART THREE

*You will hear a woman describing how her camper van was broken into. For questions 21–30, complete the notes which a newspaper reporter makes after interviewing the woman.*

# MOTORHOME ROBBERY

Motorhome parked outside | 21 _____ .

Owners had gone to collect | 22 _____

and buy | 23 _____ .

Away for about | 24 _____ .

On return found everything on floor, including

25 _____

26 _____

27 _____

28 _____

29 _____ .

Wife grabbed hold of thief.

Husband was hit in the | 30 _____ .

Nearby policeman did nothing.

Thief escaped.

## PART FOUR

*You will hear a publisher being interviewed about the possibility of a strike. She refers to the NUJ, which is a trade union – The National Union of Journalists – in which each branch is called a 'chapel'. Look at questions 31–36. Which of the statements are* TRUE *or* FALSE *according to what the woman says? Put a tick (√) in the appropriate box.*

|  | TRUE | FALSE |
|---|---|---|
| 31  The employees don't respect the managers. |  |  |
| 32  They have to work twice as hard as people in similar firms. |  |  |
| 33  Women are poorly represented in the union. |  |  |
| 34  The pay rises will only affect the men. |  |  |
| 35  They will still be underpaid even if they get a rise equal to inflation. |  |  |
| 36  The directors have awarded themselves large increases. |  |  |

## PAPER 5  INTERVIEW  (about 15 minutes)

You will be asked to take part in a theme-directed conversation with the examiner. You may be by yourself, with another candidate or with two other candidates. (Two examiners are present when there are three candidates.) The conversation will be based on one particular topic area, for example holidays, work, food.

A typical interview is described below.

★ You will be shown one, two or three photographs and invited to talk about them.

★ The examiner will then show you one or more passages and invite you to link them to the theme. You may be asked to talk a little about the content of the passage. You will *not*, however, be asked to read the passage aloud but you may quote parts of it to make your point.

★ You will then be asked to take part in a communicative activity with the other candidates present and/or the examiner (or examiners). This could involve role-play, problem solving, planning, rank ordering etc. or it could be a discussion on another aspect of the general theme of the conversation. Advertisements, diagrams and other realia are often used as stimuli here.

You will find six sample First Certificate interviews at the back of this book. Your teacher can help you to prepare for this part of the examination by assuming the role of the examiner and telling you which item in the Interview Exercises you should look at.

# Practice Test 2

## PAPER 1   READING COMPREHENSION   (1 hour)

*Answer all questions. Indicate your choice of answer in every case* **on the separate answer sheet** *already given out, which should show your name and examination index number. Follow carefully the instructions about how to record your answers. Give* **one answer only** *to each question. Marks will not be deducted for wrong answers: your total score on this test will be the number of correct answers you give.*

### SECTION A

*In this section you must choose the word or phrase which best completes each sentence.* **On your answer sheet** *indicate the letter A, B, C or D against the number of each item 1 to 25 for the word or phrase you choose.*

1   Firemen rescued several people from the ............... floor of the blazing building.
     A  high      B  top      C  basement      D  low

2   When the electricity failed, he ............... a match to find the candles.
     A  rubbed      B  scratched      C  struck      D  started

3   She put ............... speaking to him as long as possible.
     A  off      B  over      C  away      D  back

4   She wondered ............... her father looked like now, after so many years away.
     A  how      B  whose      C  that      D  what

5   She ............... her neighbour's children for the broken window.
     A  accused      B  complained      C  blamed      D  denied

6   He filled in the necessary forms and ............... for the job.
     A  appealed      B  asked      C  requested      D  applied

7   He says he's been to ............... restaurant in town.
     A  many      B  every      C  all      D  most

8   She hasn't written to me ............... .
     A  already      B  yet      C  never      D  any longer

21

9   She is travelling to work by train today because her car is being ................. .
    A stopped     B broken     C serviced     D rented

10   He tried every key in turn but not ................. fitted.
     A each     B one     C any     D none

11   Don't you get tired ................. watching TV every night?
     A with     B by     C of     D at

12   I asked Gill what time it was but she said she ................. a watch.
     A didn't get     B didn't put     C didn't have     D didn't take

13   The film lasted three hours with ................. of 15 minutes between part one
     and part two.
     A an interval     B a pause     C a stop     D an interruption

14   If you saw a lawyer, he'd ................. you to take legal action.
     A suggest     B warn     C consider     D advise

15   I'm very busy at the moment so it may take a ................. time to answer your
     letters.
     A little     B few     C small     D some

16   I've known him ................. I left college.
     A when     B during     C until     D since

17   He was wearing a heavy overcoat to ................. himself against the cold.
     A conceal     B protect     C cover     D wrap

18   It took Michael a long time to find a pair of shoes that ................. him.
     A liked     B fitted     C agreed     D matched

19   ................. the traffic was bad, I arrived on time.
     A Although     B In spite of     C Despite     D Even

20   The discovery was a major ................. for research workers.
     A breakthrough     B breakdown     C break-in     D breakout

21   ................. me to phone them before I go out.
     A Remind     B Remember     C Mention     D Make

22   He was unwilling to explain the reason ................. his absence.
     A for     B why     C of     D that

23   They wasted ................. time searching for the car keys.
     A priceless     B costly     C valuable     D expensive

24  I like to ................. the crossword puzzle in the newspaper every day.
    A fill    B make    C do    D answer

25  I find the times of English meals very strange – I'm not used ................. dinner at 6 pm.
    A to have    B to having    C having    D have

## SECTION B

*In this section you will find after each of the passages a number of questions or unfinished statements about the passage, each with four suggested answers or ways of finishing. You must choose the one which you think fits best.* **On your answer sheet, indicate the letter A, B, C or D against the number of each item 26–40 for the answer you choose. Give one answer only to each question. Read each passage right through before choosing your answers.**

FIRST PASSAGE

For the first time, ever, she had to move away from the sun. She had suffered it for an hour, only to annoy the young ones on the beach. They had made it clear, right from the start, that she was not welcome; that the beach was their playground. They reminded her of the mosquitoes that used to fly about above the river on summer evenings. She would put up with the mosquitoes, determined to finish her journey, although longing for the feel of ice-cold water on her face. She would have put up with these, too, if it hadn't been for the sun.

Now they would assume that it was they, and not the sun, that had made her leave the beach. As she sometimes ran for a bus, the rain splashing against her legs, or as she fought the wind, she was still young. Some people believed that it was the early seasons of the year that showed them at their best. She found it easier to be young in winter, when the little strength that remained within her was evident as an evergreen in an avenue of dying trees. The sun was a cruel thing, revealing one's age as it did the dust on furniture.

At the edge of the sea the middle-aged people sat in folding chairs. How pleasant it would be to set her chair among them, its cloth between her and the sun. They would accept her as one of them; would let her settle in their company. But she dragged herself past and made her way towards the benches.

There was room for one, right on the very edge. It was here that the old people sat, a long line of them, linked together like a chain. By her side sat an old woman, her dress hanging loose at her waist – an old woman, flat-chested, long and tough, like a man.

What were they looking for, she wondered, here in the middle of nowhere? Were old people greedier than they used to be? Her grandmother never went farther than the end of the road. How disappointed she would have been if grandmother had ever insisted on leaving her world. Old people should stay at home, being quietened before their own fires; guarding treasures that they had collected over the years.

She, too, should have stayed at home. But others had packed her case and pushed her on to a train.

26 She did not move off the beach earlier because
   A she was enjoying herself there.
   B she always stayed for at least an hour.
   C she knew that the young people wanted her to leave.
   D she wanted to watch the young people having fun.

27 She finally left the beach because
   A it was too crowded.
   B she had a journey to finish.
   C the mosquitoes were annoying her.
   D the sun was too hot.

28 How does she feel about the sun?
   A It makes her feel old.
   B It gives her strength.
   C It is preferable to the wind and rain.
   D It shows her at her best.

29 She thinks that old people should stay at home because
   A they find travelling too difficult.
   B they have responsibilities.
   C they might get cold.
   D they don't need new experiences.

30 Which group of people does she feel comfortable with?
   A the young people
   B the middle-aged people
   C the old people
   D none of them

31 In this passage, the woman seems to be
   A worried.
   B contented.
   C annoyed.
   D excited.

SECOND PASSAGE

Sleep is a natural process, and although a lot has been written about the subject, it is still surrounded by mystery. It is used by some as an escape from the world, and regarded by others as an irritating waste of time; some people get by on very little, others claim they cannot exist without at least ten hours; but nobody can do without sleep completely.

Our night's sleep does not just consist of a steady phase of gradually deepening sleep. It alternates between two stages: non-dreaming or ordinary sleep, and REM (rapid eye movement) or dreaming sleep.

As soon as we fall asleep we go straight into non-dreaming sleep for an hour or so, then into REM sleep for about 15 minutes, then back into non-dreaming sleep. It alternates in this way for the rest of the night, with non-dreaming sleep tending to last longer at the beginning of the night. Non-dreaming sleep occupies about three-quarters of our night's sleep, about a quarter of it deep and the rest fairly light.

It is widely believed that sleep repairs the body and makes good the damage caused by being awake. But its main function is to refresh the brain. Experts believe that probably only about two-thirds of our sleep is necessary for repairing and refreshing the brain, with the most valuable sleep coming in the first few hours of the non-dreaming period: the last few hours of sleep are not so essential. The brain can manage quite well with reduced sleep as long as it is uninterrupted sleep.

The quality of sleep is important. A study conducted in the USA looked at short sleepers, who slept for 5.5 hours on average, and long sleepers, who had 8.5 hours or more. It was discovered after a variety of tests that the long sleepers were poor sleepers, had twice as much REM sleep as the short sleepers, appeared to sleep longer to make up for poor sleep, and did not wake up in the morning refreshed. Similarly, people who sleep deeply are not necessarily getting a better quality of sleep than shallow sleepers. Deep sleepers can feel tired the following day, so six hours of good sleep is worth more than eight hours of troubled sleep.

Problems of sleeplessness generally fall into three types: 'sleep-onset insomnia', which is difficulty in getting to sleep; disturbed sleep; and early morning wakening, commonly found in elderly people over 60 who wake up in the early hours and are unable to get back to sleep again. It is the difficulty of getting to sleep which is most common among people between 40 and 50. In fact, an estimated 10% of the population worry because they are not getting enough sleep, and insomnia is one of the commonest problems doctors have to deal with.

32  According to the text, sleep is
   A  a well understood natural process.
   B  a basic human need.
   C  a poor use of valuable time.
   D  a subject for disagreement.

33  The pattern of a night's sleep is
   A  an hour of dreaming sleep followed by light sleep for the rest of the night.
   B  a 15-minute phase of REM sleep followed by ordinary sleep for the rest of the night.
   C  long periods of non-dreaming sleep interrupted by short periods of dreaming sleep.
   D  deep sleep for three-quarters of the night followed by light sleep for the rest of the night.

34  What is the most important role of sleep?
   A  It enables us to experience dreams.
   B  It enables the body to repair any damage.
   C  It divides each 24 hours into manageable periods.
   D  It offers the brain a chance to rest and recover.

35  What did the tests in the USA suggest about the quality of sleep?
   A  Six hours of sleep is better than eight hours.
   B  Deep sleepers wake more refreshed than shallow sleepers.
   C  Long sleepers need to dream more than short sleepers.
   D  The type of sleep is more important than the length.

36  'Sleep-onset insomnia' is one of the commonest sleeping problems suffered by
   A  elderly people.
   B  people between 40 and 50.
   C  10% of the population.
   D  doctors.

THIRD PASSAGE

WEST
SUSSEX
COUNTY
COUNCIL
LIBRARY SERVICE

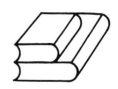

**LENDING LIBRARIES – HOW TO BORROW BOOKS & OTHER ITEMS**

1.  Anyone who lives, works or studies in West Sussex may join by completing a simple application form.
2.  The membership ticket, valid while in current use, bears your name and registration number.
3.  NO ITEM CAN BE ISSUED UNLESS THIS TICKET IS PRODUCED.

4. You may borrow up to three books or other items at any one time.

5. Each time you borrow a book, a 'light' pen 'reads' your registration number and then records each book you wish to take out by 'reading' the book number. Similarly, when you return your book, the machine will 'read' the book number and cancel the loan.

6. The ticket must be kept in a safe place. Treat it with as much care as your driving licence or credit card, and always bring it with you when you visit the library. It should only be used by the person named, who is responsible for all books borrowed on it. A charge will be made for the replacement of a lost or damaged book.

7. Provided that books are not required by another reader, they may be renewed for a further period of three weeks by either *(a)* bringing the books and your borrower's ticket to the library or *(b)* telephoning or writing to the library, stating the authors and titles of your books, the date on which the books were due back and quoting the numbers on the bar coded label. On all correspondence please quote your ticket number and relevant book numbers.

8. Fines are charged on overdue books.

9. If at any time there is a failure to comply with any of these terms, the ticket may be withdrawn.

37  As a member of the library you must
  A live in West Sussex.
  B have a ticket for each book.
  C borrow no more than three things.
  D remember your membership number.

38  We are told that the membership ticket
  A can be lent to another reader.
  B must be kept in a safe.
  C will be replaced free of charge.
  D should be brought on each visit.

39  What must you do if you want to keep books for longer than three weeks?
  A Pay extra for each day you keep them.
  B Call the library on the day the books are due.
  C Arrange it with the library personally.
  D Ask another reader to borrow them for you.

40  You have to pay when you
  A borrow books.
  B do not return books on time.
  C return books to the library.
  D complete the application form.

# PAPER 2   COMPOSITION   (1½ hours)

*Write **two only** of the following composition exercises. Your answers must follow exactly the instructions given and must be of between 120 and 180 words each.*

1   You have decided to leave your present job. Write a letter to a friend explaining why you have made this decision and what you hope to do next.

2   Local people have complained that the social club to which you belong makes too much noise, encourages bad behaviour and must therefore be closed. You have chosen to represent the club at a public meeting. What do you say?

3   On a boating holiday with a group of friends, one member of the group had an accident. Describe the accident and say what happened next.

4   'It is essential for everyone to learn one foreign language.' Do you agree?

5   Based on your reading of *one* of these books, write on **one** of the following.

   R. L. STEVENSON: *Dr Jekyll and Mr Hyde*
   Dr Lanyon left Utterson a letter which he was to read after the death of Dr Jekyll. What was Dr Lanyon's story and what happened to him after the events he described?

   MAYA ANGELOU: *I Know Why the Caged Bird Sings*
   Give some examples of the racial prejudice that white people in Stamps showed towards the black community.

   LAURIE LEE: *Cider with Rosie*
   Describe Laurie Lee's family and the kind of life they led.

# PAPER 3   USE OF ENGLISH   (2 hours)

1   *Fill each of the numbered blanks in the following passage. Use only* **one** *word in each space.*

John Lennon was born in Liverpool in 1940. He was always (1) ............................
on music and played in pop groups (2) ............................ school and Art College.

John got married (3) ............................ Cynthia in 1962 and they had a son,
(4) ............................ name was Julian. At that (5) ............................ , John was a
member of a group (6) ............................ 'The Beatles.' Many beautiful songs
(7) ............................ written by John and wherever the group went, crowds of
fans gathered to see them. They (8) ............................ scream and faint when 'The
Beatles' played, and lots of people (9) ............................ their hair cut in a Beatles
style. Soon, everyone had heard of 'The Beatles' and John was
(10) ............................ richer than he had ever (11) ............................ .

Having achieved world-wide success, John started to make records
(12) ............................ his own after 1968, and it was in the same year
(13) ............................ his marriage to Cynthia (14) ............................ to an end. He had
met Yoko Ono, a Japanese artist, (15) ............................ he married the following
year. John lost weight and grew his hair long, as can (16) ............................ seen
on the covers of the records that he made with Yoko. They (17) ............................
up home in the United States and had a son called Sean.

Many people consider John Lennon to be the most talented of all 'The
Beatles.' He sang about peace and love and so when he was murdered
(18) ............................ one of his fans, outside his New York apartment, the
(19) ............................ world was shocked. More than 50,000 fans turned
(20) ............................ to a special ceremony in his memory. He was only forty
when he died.

2   *Finish each of the following sentences in such a way that it means the same as the sentence printed before it.*

EXAMPLE:  I haven't enjoyed myself so much for years.

ANSWER:  It's years *since I enjoyed myself so much.*

a)   Henry regretted buying the second-hand car.

Henry wished ................................................................................................

b)   Amanda finally managed to get a good job.

Amanda finally succeeded ................................................................................

c)   They have sold that old house at the end of the road.

That old house ................................................................................................

d)   'Don't bite your nails,' said Mrs Rogers to her son.

Mrs Rogers told ................................................................................................

e)   Charles lives quite near his aunt's house.

Charles doesn't ................................................................................................

f)   That's the last time I go to that restaurant!

I certainly ................................................................................................

g)   It was such a dirty beach we decided not to stay.

The beach ................................................................................................

h)   It isn't necessary to finish the work today.

You don't ................................................................................................

i)   I don't really want to have lunch yet.

I'd rather ................................................................................................

j)   Sebastian's career as a television presenter began five years ago.

Sebastian has ................................................................................................

................................................................................................

3   **In sentences a) – e),** *fill each of the blanks with* **one** *suitable word beginning with* **over.**

EXAMPLE:   While the sailor was on deck, a huge wave hit the ship and he fell
       *overboard.*

a)   There was so much work at the office that the manager asked Diana to
     stay on in the evening and work ................................................ .

b)   They stayed in a beautiful hotel, in a room which ................................................
     the sea.

c)   Not many of the students at the hostel in London were British; in fact,
     most of them came from ................................................ .

d)   The car in front was going very slowly, so Alan ................................................ it.

e)   Eleanor told her mother not to expect her back until the next morning as
     she was going to stay ................................................ at a friend's house.

**In sentences f) – j),** *the word in capitals below each of the sentences can be used
to form a word that fits suitably in the blank space. Fill each blank in this way.*

EXAMPLES:   He said 'Good morning' in a most *friendly* way.       FRIEND

       My teacher *encouraged* me to take this examination.   COURAGE

f)   Sally came in so ................................................ that she woke everyone up.   NOISE

g)   Martin was very ................................................ of what he had done.       SHAME

h)   The museum does not charge for ................................................ on Sundays.
                                                                          ADMIT

i)   Our ................................................ from London to Sydney took 24 hours.       FLY

j)   The secretary was very busy all day dealing with ................................................
                                                                          ENQUIRE

4  *Make all the changes and additions necessary to produce, from the following sets of words and phrases, sentences which together make a complete letter. Note carefully from the example what kind of alterations need to be made. Write each sentence in the space provided.*

EXAMPLE:  I be very surprised / receive / letter / you this morning.

ANSWER:  *I was very surprised to receive a letter from you this morning.*

22 May 1991

Dear Julia

a)  Thank you / lovely letter, which wait / me / I return / holiday yesterday.

.................................................................................................................................

.................................................................................................................................

b)  I be glad / hear you / your husband be well and enjoy live / new house.

.................................................................................................................................

.................................................................................................................................

c)  I just have / wonderful holiday / some friends / Northern Ireland.

.................................................................................................................................

.................................................................................................................................

d)  We fly / London / Belfast and visit lots / interesting places.

.................................................................................................................................

.................................................................................................................................

e)  We spend most / time fish and walk / mountains.

.................................................................................................................................

f)  Now I be ready / go back / work / Monday.

.................................................................................................................................

g)  I look forward / see both / you / my brother's wedding / September 16th.

.................................................................................................................................

.................................................................................................................................

h)  Let's hope / weather be fine!

.................................................................................................................................

With best wishes

5   *Platform One is a new magazine for English language learners of all ages.*
    *The magazine wants to find out about its readers' tastes and interests and so is*
    *running a competition to help them choose what to include in the next issue.*
    *Read the rules for the competition below and complete the paragraphs on page 34,*
    **using the information given** *and* **giving reasons for your choices.**

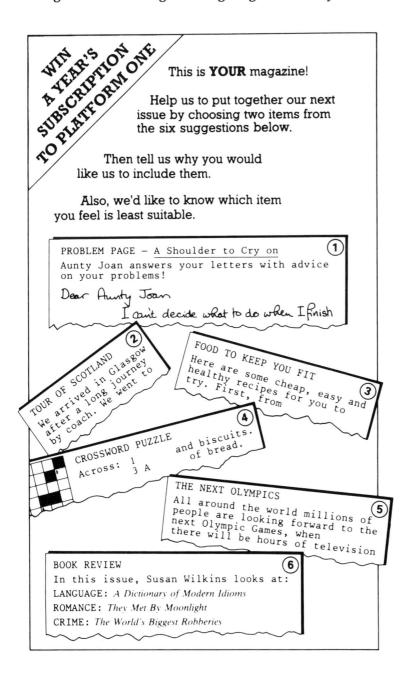

This is **YOUR** magazine!

Help us to put together our next
issue by choosing two items from
the six suggestions below.

Then tell us why you would
like us to include them.

Also, we'd like to know which item
you feel is least suitable.

> **PROBLEM PAGE** – A Shoulder to Cry on ①
> Aunty Joan answers your letters with advice
> on your problems!
> Dear Aunty Joan
>    I can't decide what to do when I finish

② TOUR OF SCOTLAND
We arrived in Glasgow
after a long journey
by coach. We went to

FOOD TO KEEP YOU FIT ③
Here are some cheap, easy and
healthy recipes for you to
try. First, from

CROSSWORD PUZZLE ④
and biscuits.
of bread.
Across: 1
        3 A

THE NEXT OLYMPICS ⑤
All around the world millions of
people are looking forward to the
next Olympic Games, when
there will be hours of television

> **BOOK REVIEW** ⑥
> In this issue, Susan Wilkins looks at:
> LANGUAGE: *A Dictionary of Modern Idioms*
> ROMANCE: *They Met By Moonlight*
> CRIME: *The World's Biggest Robberies*

a)  My first choice is .............................................................................................................

..............................................................................................................................................

..............................................................................................................................................

..............................................................................................................................................

..............................................................................................................................................

..............................................................................................................................................

..............................................................................................................................................

b)  I would also like to include .......................................................................................

..............................................................................................................................................

..............................................................................................................................................

..............................................................................................................................................

..............................................................................................................................................

..............................................................................................................................................

..............................................................................................................................................

c)  The least suitable item is .........................................................................................

..............................................................................................................................................

..............................................................................................................................................

..............................................................................................................................................

..............................................................................................................................................

..............................................................................................................................................

..............................................................................................................................................

# PAPER 4   LISTENING COMPREHENSION
## (about 30 minutes)

### PART ONE

*You will hear a woman called Melanie talking about her house.*
*For questions 1–5, decide which of the alternatives A, B, C or D is the best answer and*
*put a tick (√) in the appropriate box.*

1   How many rooms are there downstairs?

A  1 big one

B  2 small ones

C  1 big one and a small kitchen

D  1 big one, 1 small one and a kitchen

| | |
|---|---|
| A | |
| B | |
| C | |
| D | |

2   Where is the bathroom?

A  behind the kitchen

B  downstairs at the back

C  between the bedrooms

D  above the kitchen

| | |
|---|---|
| A | |
| B | |
| C | |
| D | |

3   How could Melanie tell that the previous owners had had pictures on the walls?

A  There were holes in the walls.

B  There were nails in the walls.

C  There were clean areas on the walls.

D  There were spaces between the bookshelves.

| | |
|---|---|
| A | |
| B | |
| C | |
| D | |

⟫→

4   What did Melanie do to the house during February?

|   | |
|---|---|
| A She worked hard to clean it. | A |
| B She organised the kitchen. | B |
| C She used it as an office. | C |
| D She did almost nothing. | D |

5   What did Melanie decide to do first in the kitchen?

|   | |
|---|---|
| A She decided to clean it. | A |
| B She decided to make it bigger. | B |
| C She decided to remove the cooker and cupboards. | C |
| D She decided to rearrange the cupboards. | D |

## PART TWO

*You will hear a man talking about how he runs, or **jogs**, in order to keep fit. Look at questions 6–15, decide whether the statements are TRUE or FALSE and put a tick (√) in the appropriate box.*

|   | TRUE | FALSE |
|---|---|---|
| 6   The speaker thought that 2 hours' running per week was too much. | | |
| 7   He thought the running shoes were expensive. | | |
| 8   His running shoes hurt his feet. | | |
| 9   His running shoes are nearly worn out now. | | |
| 10   He took up jogging to train for cycling. | | |
| 11   He runs regardless of the weather. | | |
| 12   He feels embarrassed about wearing shorts. | | |

|  | TRUE | FALSE |
|---|---|---|
| 13 He starts out at high speed, then slows down. |  |  |
| 14 His wife was afraid he'd fall over someone on the beach. |  |  |
| 15 He was pleased that he did not have time to start running on the beach. |  |  |

## PART THREE

*You will hear some people discussing three restaurants they have been to, called Potters, Moonshine and The Lime Tree. For questions 16–20, show how the descriptions fit the restaurants by (circling) as appropriate.*

| 16 | Cheapest: | Potters | Moonshine | The Lime Tree |
|---|---|---|---|---|
| 17 | Most expensive: | Potters | Moonshine | The Lime Tree |
| 18 | Biggest helpings: | Potters | Moonshine | The Lime Tree |
| 19 | Smallest helpings: | Potters | Moonshine | The Lime Tree |
| 20 | Old customers: | Potters | Moonshine | The Lime Tree |

## PAPER 5  INTERVIEW  (about 15 minutes)

You will be asked to take part in a theme-directed conversation with the examiner. You may be by yourself, with another candidate or with two other candidates. (Two examiners are present when there are three candidates.) The conversation will be based on one particular topic area, for example holidays, work, food.

A typical interview is described below.

★ You will be shown one, two or three photographs and invited to talk about them.

★ The examiner will then show you one or more passages and invite you to link them to the theme. You may be asked to talk a little about the content of the passage. You will *not*, however, be asked to read the passage aloud, but you may quote parts of it to make your point.

★ You will then be asked to take part in a communicative activity with the other candidates present and/or the examiner (or examiners). This could involve role-play, problem solving, planning, rank ordering etc. or it could be a discussion on another aspect of the general theme of the conversation. Advertisements, diagrams and other realia are often used as stimuli here.

You will find six sample First Certificate interviews at the back of this book. Your teacher can help you to prepare for this part of the examination by assuming the role of the examiner and telling you which item in the Interview Exercises you should look at.

# Practice Test 3

## PAPER 1   READING COMPREHENSION   (1 hour)

*Answer all questions. Indicate your choice of answer in every case* **on the separate answer sheet** *already given out, which should show your name and examination index number. Follow carefully the instructions about how to record your answers. Give* **one answer only** *to each question. Marks will not be deducted for wrong answers: your total score on this test will be the number of correct answers you give.*

### SECTION A

*In this section you must choose the word or phrase which best completes each sentence.* **On your answer sheet** *indicate the letter A, B, C or D against the number of each item 1 to 25 for the word or phrase you choose.*

1   I'm sure they were ................. lies!
    A telling      B making      C doing      D saying

2   Nobody knows what the ................. of the explosion was.
    A source      B cause      C reaction      D reason

3   Banks only ................. money if they are sure it will be paid back.
    A borrow      B lend      C interest      D charge

4   ................. of the committee, I'd like to thank you for your generous donation.
    A According      B On behalf      C Together      D In addition

5   Don't forget to ................. the alarm clock for six o'clock tomorrow morning.
    A put      B ring      C set      D wind

6   Give me a word ................. with S.
    A beginning      B begins      C began      D begin

7   After the accident, the injured cyclist was in great ................. .
    A agony      B suffering      C hurt      D pain

8   There was nothing special about his clothes ................. from his flowery tie.
    A but      B except      C other      D apart

9   Her excellent ................. in the exams helped her to find a job.
    A notes      B reports      C marks      D degrees

10  ................. stay the night if it's too difficult to get home.
    A  At all costs      B  By all means      C  In all      D  On the whole

11  ................. the step when you go in.
    A  Consider      B  Mind      C  Attend      D  Look

12  She went ................. a bad cold just before Christmas.
    A  down with      B  in for      C  over      D  through

13  It was clear that the young couple were ................. of taking charge of
    the restaurant
    A  responsible      B  reliable      C  capable      D  able

14  She used to ................. her living by delivering vegetables to local
    hotels.
    A  earn      B  gain      C  get      D  win

15  I'm absolutely no good at all ................. any kind of sport.
    A  with      B  on      C  at      D  for

16  That sweater looks ................. small for a five-year-old.
    A  bit      B  much      C  rather      D  even

17  Since I moved house, I haven't had much ................. with those friends.
    A  connection      B  contact      C  business      D  meeting

18  I'd rather you ................. to her why we can't go.
    A  would explain      B  explained      C  to explain      D  will explain

19  I looked up their number in the telephone ................. .
    A  guide      B  list      C  directory      D  catalogue

20  I'd have told you if I ................. the book.
    A  had seen      B  should have seen      C  saw      D  would have seen

21  In the old days, people believed that the world was flat and ships would
    fall off the ................. .
    A  boundary      B  edge      C  border      D  limit

22  They had never come ................. such a beautiful little village before.
    A  off      B  along      C  at      D  across

23  There weren't any ................. in the factory for bilingual secretaries.
    A  situations      B  spaces      C  vacancies      D  offers

24  Unfortunately his illness turned out to be extremely ................. so he was kept in isolation.
    A influential    B infectious    C individual    D inoffensive

25  What ................. milk shake do you want – strawberry, chocolate, or orange?
    A taste    B kind    C flavour    D type


## SECTION B

*In this section you will find after each of the passages a number of questions or unfinished statements about the passage, each with four suggested answers or ways of finishing. You must choose the one which you think fits best.* **On your answer sheet, indicate the letter A, B, C or D against the number of each item 26–40 for the answer you choose. Give** **one answer only** *to each question. Read each passage right through before choosing your answers.*


FIRST PASSAGE

I had feared that my companion would talk, but it was soon plain that there was no such danger. Two days passed during which we did not exchange a single word. He seemed, indeed, absolutely unaware of my presence. He neither read nor wrote, but spent most of his time sitting at the table and looking out of the window across the pleasant parkland that surrounded the house. He sometimes talked to himself and said things half under his breath. He bit his nails and once he produced a penknife and dug holes in the furniture until one of the attendants took it from him. I thought at first that perhaps he was mentally ill. During the second day I even began to feel a little nervous of him. He was extremely large, both broad and tall, with very wide shoulders and enormous hands. His huge head was usually sunk low between his shoulders. He had dark, rather untidy hair and a big, shapeless mouth, which opened every now and then. Once or twice he began singing to himself, but broke off abruptly on each occasion – and this was the nearest he seemed to get to noticing my presence.

By the evening of the second day I was completely unable to go on with my work. Out of a mixture of nervousness and curiosity, I sat too looking out of my window, and blowing my nose, and wondering how to set about establishing the human contact which was by now becoming an absolute necessity. It ended up with my asking him for his name. He had been introduced to me when he arrived, but I had paid no attention then. He turned towards me a very gentle pair of dark eyes and said his name: Hugo Belfounder. He added: 'I thought you didn't want to talk.' I said that I was not at all against talking, that I had just been rather busy with something when he arrived, and I begged his pardon if I had appeared rude. It seemed to me, even from the way he spoke, that he was not only not mentally ill, but was highly intelligent; and I began, almost automatically, to pack up my papers. I knew that from now on I should do no more work. I was sharing a room with a person of the greatest fascination.

26  How did Hugo spend the first two days?
    A  He talked and sang to himself from time to time.
    B  He spent his time making holes in the furniture.
    C  He worked as if the writer was not there.
    D  He kept annoying the attendants.

27  On the second evening, the writer
    A  tried in vain to start a conversation.
    B  began to feel frightened of his companion.
    C  could not concentrate on his work.
    D  was feeling bored.

28  Hugo did not talk to the writer at first because
    A  he did not realise the writer wished to.
    B  he was feeling ill.
    C  he was too busy.
    D  he thought the writer was rude.

29  The writer's attitude to Hugo changed from
    A  fear to nervousness.
    B  curiosity to nervousness.
    C  nervousness to unfriendliness.
    D  nervousness to interest.

SECOND PASSAGE

Before man had flown in space it was thought that his physical and mental capabilities might be affected by long periods of weightlessness, and that he might be endangered by high levels of radiation. Yuri Gagarin's first space flight in April 1961 showed that man could live in space and, although this journey only lasted for 108 minutes, it gave encouragement to those interested in the future of manned space flight. In fact most of the early fears about man's health in space have proved groundless, and although several odd medical effects have been observed, none has seriously affected man's ability for useful work. All astronauts undergo strenuous training to prepare them for the experience of space flight but, despite this, most astronauts suffer from space sickness early in their flights. This effect, similar to sea sickness, soon wears off, and there appears to be no medical reason why man cannot live in space for long periods of time. A constant check is kept on the health of all astronauts during their mission. Small medical detectors which monitor their heartbeats, pulse rates, breathing and temperature are taped to their bodies.

All food eaten in space so far has been prepared on earth. The alternative possibilities of making food from waste products or growing it in space have received little serious consideration. The first space foods were simply baby foods. In the first American space flights, astronauts ate natural foods in dried bite-sized squares or in a form that could be mixed with cold water and squeezed into the mouth. The squares were coated to prevent them breaking up into small pieces, and their corners were rounded to prevent them cutting the astronauts' mouths. Later astronauts ate 'sticky' foods with a spoon, and hot as well as cold water was available for making up the dried meals. These two developments have made eating in space much more pleasant.

30  Yuri Gagarin's first space flight showed
    A  scientists could develop weapons in space.
    B  human beings could survive well in space.
    C  astronauts would not suffer from space sickness.
    D  all the scientific equipment worked well.

31  How is the health of human beings affected in space?
    A  The effects can be unpleasant but harmless.
    B  There is a slight risk of heart problems.
    C  Longer space flights are more dangerous to health.
    D  Space sickness lasts throughout the flight.

32  What do we learn of early space food?
    A  It was surprisingly tasty.
    B  The edges cut the astronauts' mouths.
    C  It was eaten cold.
    D  It was inconvenient because it dissolved.

33  How has space food improved since the first space flights?
    A  Baby food has been cut from the diet.
    B  The food is now produced in bite-sized squares.
    C  Some normal food is now available.
    D  There is a greater variety of foods available.

THIRD PASSAGE

Like so many other materials in Japan, paper too has come in for many hundreds of years of artistic consideration. At one period of the country's history, the paper on which a poem was written was as important as the poem itself. A thousand years ago there were whole towns actively engaged in making paper. Such towns still exist, but there were also many farming villages which then, as they do today, made paper to earn extra income during the winter. At present, about half of Japan's farmers must add to their incomes with winter jobs. Although a large amount of winter employment is provided by construction companies, some farmers continue to work at such cottage industries as paper-making.

The farmer who makes paper may interrupt his work at any point to perform other jobs in the home and the fields. For both farmer and professional, sun, wind, and running water are necessary. And because nature is not always reliable, it too may interrupt the process of paper-making. These factors cause, day by day, month by month, and year by year, the small variations in colour and quality of handmade paper. A keen sensitivity to the small differences of weather, growing cycles, purity of water, quality of plants, duration of a snowfall, and temperature is required. This is learnt over many years of living close to nature.

The romantic ideas associated with paper become less so when one realises the amount of demanding physical work that goes into its making. Much of the paper-maker's time is spent outdoors in the snow. Putting up with the cold is the most difficult but not the only cause of suffering. The paper-maker works long hours, about ten a day, with hands in icy water, taking no vacations, and making just enough money to exist on. Constant reminders of the results of this work are sore hands, painful wounds, and stiffness and swelling that lasts all year round. The paper-maker who continues to work under these circumstances may be likened to an artist who in search of art doesn't pay any attention to hard conditions. It takes ten years to learn this art, and today it is largely practised by women, for the men of the paper-making family handle the business matters.

34  Who in Japan today earns extra money by making paper?
    A  the majority of Japanese farmers
    B  people who also work for construction companies
    C  fewer than half of Japan's farmers
    D  the inhabitants of certain towns

35  The colour and quality of handmade paper vary because
    A  there may be unexpected changes in weather.
    B  it takes such a long time to make.
    C  the process can often be interrupted.
    D  the farmer may not have much experience.

36  What do we learn about paper-making?
    A  It is hard outdoor work.
    B  It requires artistic skills.
    C  It is a highly profitable business.
    D  It is performed all year round.

FOURTH PASSAGE

# FARMHOUSE HOLIDAYS

---

Mrs AUDREY M HODGE, Kevley, 20 Southey Street, Keswick, AC12 4EF.
Tel: Keswick (596) 73455

---

A small, comfortable guest house where good food and cleanliness are guaranteed. Situated conveniently for shops and parks and 10 minutes' walk from the lake. All bedrooms heated, have hot and cold water, tea-making facilities and all beds with spring interior mattresses and electric blankets. Packed lunches are available upon request. A light supper served at 10.15 pm. Two double rooms, all with washbasins, bathroom, two toilets, sitting room, dining room. Sorry no pets. Car not essential but parking space. Fire Certificate granted. Evening Meal, Bed and Breakfast or Bed and Breakfast only. SAE please or telephone for terms.

---

Mr and Mrs JOHN CHASE, Lynwood, 211 Ambleside Road, Keswick.
Tel: (596) 72081.

---

Lynwood is a friendly 130-year-old guest house in the heart of the Lake District. Quietly situated five minutes' walk from the town centre and ten minutes' walk from the lakeside. All our comfortable bedrooms have tea/coffee makers, electric blankets, hot and cold water and shaver points. Access at all times. Lynwood has drying facilities and bicycles available for hire. Full central heating and Fire Certificate, TV lounge, AA and RAC listed. We offer excellent food and wines and a high standard of comfort and personal attention. Residents' licence. Sorry no pets or children under 8 years. Open most of the year including Christmas. Brochure on request.

---

Mrs M M POTTER, Birkrigg Farm, Newside, Keswick, AC12 5TS.
Tel: Braithwaite (596-821) 278.

---

Birkrigg is a dairy cattle and sheep farm pleasantly and peacefully situated in a valley surrounded by mountains. Ideal for walking and climbing. Five miles from Keswick and three from Buttermere. A mini-bus service operates between the two, passing the farm several times daily. A car is essential if wishing to tour the many beauty spots. Parking space. Clean, comfortable accommodation comprises one single, two double, and two family rooms, all with washbasins, shaver points. Bathroom, toilet, sitting room with colour TV, dining room. Good meals assured. Children welcome at reduced rates. Babysitting for children over 5. Bed and Breakfast, Evening Dinners available five nights of the week. Evening tea 10 pm. Open late March early November. Fire Certificate held. Terms on request. SAE please.

>>>→

Mrs E M DIXON, Fold Head Farm, Watendlath, Borrowdale, Keswick.
Tel: Borrowdale (59-684) 255.

Fold Head Farmhouse is a white lakeland farmhouse situated in this picturesque hamlet. It is a 3,000 acre sheep farm and an ideal centre for touring, climbing, fell walking and fishing. Guests are accommodated in three double bedrooms and two family rooms, with washbasins, bathroom, two toilets, sitting room, dining room. Children are welcome and there is a cot and babysitting. Pets are allowed by arrangement, free. Open from February to December. Car parking space available. Sir Hugh Walpole used this farmhouse in his book 'Judith Patts' as the home of Judith Patts. Evening Dinner, Bed and Breakfast or Bed and Breakfast. Rates reduced for children. SAE for further details.

37  You don't own a car but you wish to spend a holiday in the Lake District. Which place would be unsuitable?
    A 1     B 2     C 3     D 4

38  You have a small baby but enjoy going out in the evenings. Where would you go?
    A 1     B 2     C 3     D 4

39  Families wanting evening dinner every day should avoid
    A 1     B 2     C 3     D 4

40  If you were passing through the area in January and wanted somewhere to stay, which two places would it be worth phoning?
    A 1 and 2     B 1 and 4     C 2 and 3     D 3 and 4

# PAPER 2   COMPOSITION   (1½ hours)

*Write **two only** of the following composition exercises. Your answers must follow exactly the instructions given and must be of between 120 and 180 words each.*

1   You have just started a new job. Write a letter to a friend or relative describing your first week at work. Explain what your future career plans are.

2   You have just witnessed a road traffic accident and the police have asked you to make a statement describing exactly what happened. Write what you say.

3   Write a story about an occasion when you were able to help somebody to solve a problem.

4   'People in many countries watch too much television these days.' Do you agree?

5   Based on your reading of *one* of these books, write on **one** of the following.

R. L. STEVENSON: *Dr Jekyll and Mr Hyde*
Explain why Dr Jekyll made two wills, leaving his possessions first to Edward Hyde and later to Mr Utterson.

MAYA ANGELOU: *I Know Why the Caged Bird Sings*
Explain how Maya and her brother came to live with their grandmother in Stamps, Arkansas, as very young children, and describe their early life there.

LAURIE LEE: *Cider with Rosie*
'Our village school was poor and crowded, but in the end I loved it.'
Describe some of Laurie Lee's experiences of school life.

# PAPER 3   USE OF ENGLISH   (2 hours)

1   *Fill each of the numbered blanks in the following passage. Use only* **one** *word in each space.*

It was the day of my grandmother's 80th birthday when the sitting-room ceiling fell down. All the family were there, at my Uncle Philip's house, (1) .............................. was a large, old building situated in a small, peaceful village north-west (2) .............................. Oxford. We (3) .............................. already finished lunch and, as (4) .............................. was such a beautiful afternoon, we were all outside (5) .............................. the garden, drinking coffee and catching (6) .............................. on all the family news. Grandmother, (7) .............................. was rather deaf, was (8) .............................. usual, telling stories about her childhood in Manchester, (9) .............................. in the sunshine, laughing children and barking dogs chased each (10) .............................. around.

Suddenly, (11) .............................. was a tremendous crash. We all looked round in astonishment, wondering what on earth had (12) .............................. . Uncle Philip and my father ran into the house, and then my sister and I (13) .............................. . There, the most extraordinary sight met our eyes. The sitting-room was (14) .............................. ruins and the air was thick with dust. Uncle Philip (15) .............................. standing in the (16) .............................. of the room, holding Tabatha, his cat, who looked terrified. 'It's (17) .............................. of the problems of living in a house as old (18) .............................. this,' he explained calmly. Meanwhile, outside, Grandmother asked (19) .............................. more coffee and enquired when the cake (20) .............................. be cut.

2   *Finish each of the following sentences in such a way that it means the same as the sentence printed before it.*

EXAMPLE: I haven't enjoyed myself so much for years.

ANSWER:  It's years *since I enjoyed myself so much.*

a)  That meal was excellent!

   What ...............................................................................................................................

b)  'I've seen the film three times, Mary,' said George.

   George told ...................................................................................................................

c)  I don't really want to visit the museum.

   I'd rather .......................................................................................................................

d)  John missed the ferry because his car broke down.

   If .....................................................................................................................................

e)  Jane is a better cook than Robert.

   Robert can't ..................................................................................................................

f)  Please do not smoke in this area of the restaurant.

   Customers are requested ...........................................................................................

   ..........................................................................................................................................

g)  'I'm sorry, Angela,' said Martin, 'I'm afraid I've damaged your car.'

   Martin apologised .......................................................................................................

h)  Although he took a taxi, Bill still arrived late for the concert.

   In spite ..........................................................................................................................

   ..........................................................................................................................................

i)  Carol finds it easy to make friends.

   Carol has no ..................................................................................................................

j)  Mark is too young to see the horror film.

   Mark is not ...................................................................................................................

3   *The word in capitals below each of the following sentences can be used to form a word that fits suitably in the blank space. Fill each blank in this way.*

EXAMPLES:  He said 'Good morning' in a most *friendly* way.   FRIEND

My teacher *encouraged* me to take this examination.   COURAGE

a)   The country is very ............................................... so travelling by road is difficult.   MOUNTAIN

b)   The teacher stressed the need for regular ............................................... .   ATTEND

c)   Sarah ............................................... opened the door of the cellar, wondering what she might find.   CAUTION

d)   There were over fifty ............................................... in the orchestra.   MUSIC

e)   Jim always does what he says; he's a very ............................................... person.   RELY

f)   Alexander knows which mushrooms are ............................................... , so ask him before you pick them.   POISON

g)   The company is very efficient and gives a ............................................... service.   SPEED

h)   The ............................................... of the fire was very welcome after our long walk.   WARM

i)   They have agreed to ............................................... the road because of the amount of heavy traffic now using it.   WIDE

j)   John's ............................................... improved at his new school.   BEHAVE

4   *Make all the changes and additions necessary to produce, from the following sets of words and phrases, sentences which together make a complete letter from a teacher replying to an invitation. Note carefully from the example what kind of alterations need to be made. Write each sentence in the space provided.*

EXAMPLE:  I be very surprised / receive / letter / you this morning.

ANSWER:   *I was very surprised to receive a letter from you this morning.*

9 May 1991

Dear Mr Harris

a)  I be very pleased / meet you / teachers' conference / London last year.

    ............................................................................................................................

    ............................................................................................................................

b)  It be kind / you / invite me / come and see you while I be / England / this summer.

    ............................................................................................................................

    ............................................................................................................................

c)  I hope / pay a visit / your school / 26th and 27th June if / not be inconvenient.

    ............................................................................................................................

    ............................................................................................................................

d)  Please / not rearrange / programme / me.

    ............................................................................................................................

e)  I be very happy / fit in / whatever you / do at that time.

    ............................................................................................................................

    ............................................................................................................................

f)  I like / stay overnight / 26th June and hope / arrange accommodation / me.

    ............................................................................................................................

    ............................................................................................................................

g)  I telephone you once / reach London / confirm / exact time / arrival / school.

    ............................................................................................................................

    ............................................................................................................................

h)  I look forward / meet / again.

    ............................................................................................................................

Yours sincerely

5 *Radford is a small industrial town without many facilities for its growing population. You are a member of the local council, which is meeting to decide how to use an empty site near the centre of the town. The four most popular ideas for the development are given below.* **Using the information given**, *complete the paragraphs on page 53,* **giving reasons for your choices**.

a) I am most in favour of ................................................................................................................................

................................................................................................................................................................

................................................................................................................................................................

................................................................................................................................................................

................................................................................................................................................................

................................................................................................................................................................

................................................................................................................................................................

b) My second choice would be ................................................................................................................

................................................................................................................................................................

................................................................................................................................................................

................................................................................................................................................................

................................................................................................................................................................

................................................................................................................................................................

................................................................................................................................................................

c) However, I would not ............................................................................................................................

................................................................................................................................................................

................................................................................................................................................................

................................................................................................................................................................

................................................................................................................................................................

................................................................................................................................................................

................................................................................................................................................................

# PAPER 4   LISTENING COMPREHENSION
## (about 30 minutes)

### PART ONE

*You will hear a man talking to a class of young children just before the school
holidays, telling them about possible dangers.*
*For questions 1–8, look at the drawings, which represent possible dangers.* (Circle) YES
*or* NO *to show which the speaker mentions.*

1   YES / NO

2   YES / NO

3   YES / NO

4   YES / NO

5   YES / NO

6   YES / NO

7   YES / NO

8   YES / NO

## PART TWO

*A young boy called Paul is going into hospital next Thursday. The hospital worker is telling him what will happen.*
*For questions 9–16, look at the list of activities and put them in the correct order. The first one has been done for you as an example.*

| ACTIVITY | | THE CORRECT ORDER | |
|---|---|---|---|
| A | come into hospital | example | C |
| B | have a bath | 9 | |
| C | have breakfast | 10 | |
| D | put a bracelet on | 11 | |
| E | go to the ward | 12 | |
| F | see the doctor | 13 | |
| G | be weighed and measured | 14 | |
| H | drink medicine | 15 | |
| I | take your clothes off | 16 | |

## PART THREE

*In this part you will hear the report of an accident.*
*For questions 17–21, complete the form below with the missing information.*

---

### ACCIDENT REPORT

Date of Accident: | 17 |

Time of Accident: | 18 |

Place of Accident: ....High Street....

....Weston....

Description of Car: | 19 |

Estimated Speed of Car: | 20 |

Telephone Number of Police Station: | 21 |

---

# PAPER 5 INTERVIEW (about 15 minutes)

You will be asked to take part in a theme-directed conversation with the examiner. You may be by yourself, with another candidate or with two other candidates. (Two examiners are present when there are three candidates.) The conversation will be based on one particular topic area, for example holidays, work, food.

A typical interview is described below.

★ You will be shown one, two or three photographs and invited to talk about them.

★ The examiner will then show you one or more passages and invite you to link them to the theme. You may be asked to talk a little about the content of the passage. You will *not*, however, be asked to read the passage aloud, but you may quote parts of it to make your point.

★ You will then be asked to take part in a communicative activity with the other candidates present and/or the examiner (or examiners). This could involve role-play, problem solving, planning, rank ordering etc. or it could be a discussion on another aspect of the general theme of the conversation. Advertisements, diagrams and other realia are often used as stimuli here.

You will find six sample First Certificate interviews at the back of this book. Your teacher can help you to prepare for this part of the examination by assuming the role of the examiner and telling you which item in the Interview Exercises you should look at.

# Practice Test 4

## PAPER 1   READING COMPREHENSION   (1 hour)

*Answer all questions. Indicate your choice of answer in every case* **on the separate answer sheet** *already given out, which should show your name and examination index number. Follow carefully the instructions about how to record your answers. Give* **one answer only** *to each question. Marks will not be deducted for wrong answers: your total score on this test will be the number of correct answers you give.*

### SECTION A

*In this section you must choose the word or phrase which best completes each sentence.* **On your answer sheet** *indicate the letter A, B, C or D against the number of each item 1 to 25 for the word or phrase you choose.*

1   She always .................. the crossword in the paper before breakfast.
    A  makes      B  writes      C  does      D  works

2   When the tenants failed to pay their bill, the authorities decided to cut
    .................. the gas supply to the flat.
    A  down      B  out      C  across      D  off

3   His parents agreed to .................. him their car while they were away on
    holiday.
    A  borrow      B  lend      C  hire      D  let

4   Several items of .................. were found on the river bank.
    A  clothes      B  dress      C  costume      D  clothing

5   She had no .................. of selling the clock – it had belonged to her grandfather.
    A  intention      B  meaning      C  interest      D  opinion

6   The lake contained .................. thousands of fish.
    A  much      B  one      C  many      D  few

7   Cut the cake into six .................. pieces.
    A  same      B  like      C  alike      D  equal

8   You can use my bicycle .................. you bring it back tomorrow.
    A  as long as      B  although      C  nevertheless      D  in spite of

58

9  My brother always ................ at cards. No wonder he won every game!
   A cheated    B lied    C tricked    D deceived

10  He was so tired he wasn't capable ................ driving himself home.
    A to    B for    C of    D from

11  Fill in the form as indicated and return in the envelope ................ .
    A provided    B offered    C prepared    D given

12  If we hurry, we might get there ................ to catch the early train.
    A right    B in time    C on time    D before time

13  Our neighbours are very ................ on camping holidays.
    A eager    B enthusiastic    C interested    D keen

14  The mosquito bite made my eyelid ................ and I couldn't open my eye properly.
    A swell    B grow    C stretch    D spread

15  I had to wear ................ uniform when I worked in the hotel.
    A a    B some    C any    D an

16  I tried to ................ them from going, but they wouldn't take any notice.
    A warn    B refuse    C forbid    D prevent

17  The doctor advised me not to take ................ so much work in future.
    A after    B on    C over    D to

18  If he phones, ................ him to buy some potatoes on the way home.
    A remember    B recall    C remind    D recollect

19  Who was the first person ................ the South Pole?
    A reaching    B who reaches    C to reach    D reached

20  The ................ of the murderer lasted six weeks.
    A process    B trial    C charge    D conviction

21  A chicken can ................ up to three eggs a day.
    A lie    B lay    C put    D place

22  The nurse was on ................ in the hospital all night.
    A work    B alarm    C duty    D service

23  I suggest we ................ outside the cinema tomorrow at 8.30.
    A meeting    B meet    C met    D will meet

24 ................ playing professional basketball, she also enjoys tennis.
    A Besides    B Moreover    C Apart    D Together

25 She ................ him of lying to her.
    A threatened    B blamed    C criticised    D accused

## SECTION B

*In this section you will find after each of the passages a number of questions or unfinished statements about the passage, each with four suggested answers or ways of finishing. You must choose the one which you think fits best according to the passage.* **On your answer sheet,** *indicate the letter A, B, C or D against the number of each item 26 to 40 for the answer you choose. Give* **one answer only** *to each question. Read each passage right through before choosing your answers.*

FIRST PASSAGE

While Edward was looking through his father's private papers and unfinished drawings, he suddenly realised how badly he was behaving. He jumped up, put the papers back on the desk and made for the staircase.

When he reached the next floor he saw at once that everything was different: the space had been divided up and what Edward could see had the air of the entrance hall of a flat. The floor was carpeted and an open door revealed a bathroom. There was a small table between two closed doors. The carpet was clean, the table dusted. Edward opened a door into a kitchen, and another into a sitting room. The next door which he tried refused to open. Edward pushed it and rattled it a little, then saw that there was a key in the keyhole. The door was evidently locked on the outside. He turned the key and opened the door. The room was a bedroom. The bed was opposite the door, and lying upon the bed, raised up by his pillows, was a bearded man, looking straight at Edward with dark round eyes.

Edward thought later on that in a second of complete shock he had understood everything. He certainly came, very soon after, to understand much. He moved into the room, closing the door behind him. The man on the bed kept staring at him intently and moving his lips. His face expressed an intense emotion which Edward thought of afterwards, perhaps at the time, as a kind of apologetic anxiety which was also expressive of deep grief. Edward, shaking with emotion, approached the bed and stopped. The red lips moved, but no sound came. The large eyes begged Edward to hear, to respond. At last a sound came out which, heard together with that expression, seemed like a question. Edward grasped the sound. It was an attempt at his own name. He said, 'Edward. Yes, I am Edward. I am your son.' The helpless lips moved, as if to smile, and a shaking hand was outstretched. Edward took the weak white hand in his. Then he knelt down beside the bed and buried his face in the blanket. He felt the other hand touch his hair. He burst into tears.

26 What did Edward see at the top of the staircase?
   A an unfurnished entrance area
   B a bathroom with a carpeted floor
   C a sitting room leading into a kitchen
   D an entrance hall with several doors off it

27 How did Edward get into the bedroom?
   A He forced the door open.
   B He went through the kitchen.
   C Someone unlocked the door from the other side.
   D He unlocked the door himself.

28 How did Edward react when he saw the old man on the bed?
   A He was filled with surprise.
   B He rushed towards him.
   C He wanted to leave the room.
   D He felt frightened and angry.

29 What was the man's reaction when Edward came in?
   A He was not pleased to see him.
   B He began to whisper to himself.
   C He seemed afraid of him.
   D He tried hard to speak to him.

30 What did Edward do?
   A He shook his father's hand.
   B He began to cry.
   C He sat down on the bed.
   D He stroked his father's hair.

## SECOND PASSAGE

Are we being served? More than two thirds of those questioned in a recent survey think service in Britain's shops is not good enough and would pay more for better treatment. The disappearance of personal service is not new. Our present dissatisfaction began at least 40 years ago. When goods were scarce there was time to take pleasure in the complicated art of selling, from greeting the customer to wrapping goods. The end of the war, and the scarcity of goods which accompanied the wartime period, changed all that. People wanted choice and quantity, to help themselves to what was on offer. Self-service was born.

Throughout the Sixties and Seventies, productivity was the important word. In shops, goods were piled up to ensure bigger sales. Supermarkets grew larger, assistants scarcer. The customer, by contrast, shrank beneath the enormous piles of goods, pushed by the sound of the background music towards the check-out.

At the end of the Seventies, however, owners of the larger stores thought again. The customer was becoming more aware of what was on offer. Spending power had moved to younger people with higher expectations from their hours of shopping. Design consultants were called in and through the high street swept newly-designed stores and goods. The customer benefited, no doubt about it, but look at any row of high street shops from the north to the south of Britain. They all look the same. They offer similar ranges of goods on similarly colour-coordinated shop-fittings.

The amusing thing is that market forces may be driving shops back to the first principles of selling. In an attempt to be different from the competition, many of them are examining the quality of personal service. According to retail research analysts, customer care programmes are an important competitive weapon. Already, a number of big British companies have started new schemes. Edward Whitefield, who advises companies on selling, says that about 50 of Britain's top 500 companies are now trying to improve their customer service. Many more, he believes, will follow.

31  A recent survey showed that about one third of those questioned
  A  were satisfied with the shop service in Britain.
  B  would pay higher prices for better service.
  C  thought the service in Britain could be much better.
  D  thought that personal service had disappeared.

32  It appears that, after the end of the war, customers
  A  wanted better service from shopkeepers.
  B  disliked the idea of everyone helping themselves in shops.
  C  discovered that some goods were becoming scarcer.
  D  lost interest in personal service.

33  During the Sixties and Seventies, store owners were mainly concerned with
  A  a better choice for the customer.
  B  the amount of goods sold.
  C  the type of assistants employed.
  D  the type of music played in their shops.

34  By the end of the Seventies, however, store owners had decided to make shopping
  A  easier for young people.
  B  available at all hours.
  C  a pleasanter experience.
  D  the same in all stores.

35 Many large companies realise that better customer service
   A will increase competition.
   B benefits smaller stores.
   C attracts more business.
   D improves the quality of goods.

## THIRD PASSAGE

Our first surprise when we arrived at our holiday destination in the Dordogne in France was the welcome we received from the artists who owned the cottage we had rented. We went to pick up the key from them and were sat down in their garden and given wine and biscuits and made to feel very much at home.

Our second surprise, on being taken to our holiday house two miles away, was to find a delightful 17th century cottage – complete with antique furniture – very different from the basic houses we have stayed in on previous French holidays.

The beautiful cottage was in a village 20 miles east of Bergerac and about three miles from the busy little town of Lalinde. The Dordogne is a very popular part of France for English tourists and one cannot go far without meeting another English car. However, in the little hillside village of Couze we felt truly in France. One of my pleasures in the morning was to wander up the road to the baker's, exchanging comments with the locals, most of whom had been born in the village. They were all very welcoming and happy to chat.

The attractions of the Dordogne are well-known, but they deserve their reputation. Towns such as Sarlat and Domme are incredibly beautiful with their medieval stone buildings, and the view from the heights of Rocamadour is breath-taking. In all the popular towns it is easy to escape from the main roads, which have been commercialised, and wander in the flower-filled back streets.

Castles and fortified towns built by both the French and the English are a constant reminder of the Hundred Years' War – now seeming attractive rather than threatening. There are many riverside beaches and lakes where one can swim. Boats can be hired for a journey down the Dordogne river and sightseeing everywhere is cheap, with low charges for entrances to castles and caves and few car parking charges.

The many restaurants are also an attraction of the area with their specialties of pâté, duck and goose, and regional wines. You can pay anything from about £4.50 each for a full though basic meal, but you can have a good meal with wine for an average of £9 each. There are, of course, some superb – and delightful – restaurants where for £20–£30 per person you can have a feast!

We have booked our holiday through *Vacances* who have a most attractive selection of properties throughout France, ranging from seaside cottages in Brittany to farmhouses in the Ardèche.

By Liz Oliver.

Liz Oliver obviously enjoyed her stay at Le Château (D19) in the Dordogne – and now we'd like to hear your account of an enjoyable *Vacances* holiday. The best article,

which should be no longer than 400 words, will be published in a following issue of
*Vacances News* and there's a prize of two bottles of champagne.

36  When the writer first arrived in the Dordogne she was surprised
    A  to find the owners of their holiday cottage were artistic.
    B  to find the owners also rented other holiday cottages.
    C  by the wine and food left in the holiday cottage by the owners.
    D  by the friendliness of the owners of their holiday cottage.

37  The cottage which the writer had rented was
    A  two miles away from a house they had previously rented.
    B  next door to the bakery.
    C  situated on a hillside in a small village.
    D  twenty miles away from the nearest village.

38  Each morning when the writer took a walk, she
    A  saw English cars along the road.
    B  got into conversation with the local inhabitants.
    C  spent a long time talking to the local baker.
    D  admired the flowers in the back streets.

39  The only criticism the writer makes of the area is
    A  the constant reminders of the Hundred Years' War.
    B  the lack of car parks.
    C  the high cost of the food.
    D  the effects of tourism on some town centres.

40  The holiday company asks readers to
    A  take part in a competition.
    B  book a holiday at Le Château in the Dordogne.
    C  buy the next issue of *Vacances News*.
    D  write and ask for two free bottles of champagne.

# PAPER 2   COMPOSITION   (1½ hours)

*Write **two only** of the following composition exercises. Your answers must follow exactly the instructions given and must be of between 120 and 180 words each.*

1   You and some friends have recently had a meal in an expensive restaurant. Write a letter to the manager of the restaurant praising the food but complaining about the service.

2   You are looking after a small child and she has asked you to tell her about your own childhood when you were her age. Write down what you tell her.

3   Describe a visit to a street market where you bought something unusual.

4   Nowadays many people are worried about pollution. What do you think can be done about this world-wide problem?

5   Based on your reading of *one* of these books, write on **one** of the following.

R. L. STEVENSON: *Dr Jekyll and Mr Hyde*
Tell the story of Dr Jekyll and Mr Hyde as if you were Poole, the butler.

MAYA ANGELOU: *I Know Why the Caged Bird Sings*
Describe Maya's graduation ceremony and say why it did not turn out as happily for her as she had expected.

LAURIE LEE: *Cider with Rosie*
What changes in village and family life did Laurie Lee experience as he grew up?

# PAPER 3   USE OF ENGLISH   (2 hours)

1   *Fill each of the numbered blanks in the following passage. Use only* **one** *word in each space.*

Victor Lustig was a man who made his living by making people believe things that were not true in order to get money from them. He (1) ............................ his name twenty-four times in his career to avoid identification and was arrested forty-seven times. He did many amazing things but perhaps the (2) ............................ incredible was (3) ............................ he tried to sell the Eiffel Tower. He (4) ............................ to be a senior civil servant and invited offers (5) ............................ the Tower, based on the value of the metal when it (6) ............................ been pulled down. The man (7) ............................ offer was accepted was (8) ............................ embarrassed to make (9) ............................ fuss and Lustig, (10) ............................ had made a lot of money from the deal, walked free.

   Next he went on to try (11) ............................ luck in America. In Oklahoma, he met a sheriff and sold him a machine supposed to be (12) ............................ of making thousand-dollar bills. The unfortunate sheriff was arrested for using illegal bills, but once again, Lustig (13) ............................ to get away. Then he went to Chicago, (14) ............................ he tried to trick the gangster Al Capone into (15) ............................ him fifty thousand dollars. However, he did not (16) ............................ and Capone's men soon showed him the door.

   The American Secret Service were the people who finally brought him (17) ............................ justice. They investigated Lustig and his affairs after he had tried to cheat the US government. Lustig was (18) ............................ to prison and it was there that he died in 1947. On his (19) certificate, his occupation was described (20) ............................ 'Apprentice Salesman'.

2 *Finish each of the following sentences in such a way that it means the same as the sentence printed before it.*

EXAMPLE:  I haven't enjoyed myself so much for years.

ANSWER:   It's years *since I enjoyed myself so much.*

a)  Whose documents are these?

Who ..............................................................................................................

b)  'Have you had enough for lunch?' the landlady asked me.

The landlady asked ....................................................................................

c)  We ought to leave the party now if we are to catch the last train.

If we don't ..................................................................................................

..............................................................................................................

d)  It's Alice's job to look after new staff.

Alice is responsible ....................................................................................

e)  What's your date of birth?

When ............................................................................................................

f)  John could not find the right house.

John was ......................................................................................................

g)  The doctor should have signed my insurance form.

My insurance form ....................................................................................

..............................................................................................................

h)  Michael laughed when I told him the joke.

The joke ......................................................................................................

i)  Jenny does not play tennis as well as she used to.

Jenny used ..................................................................................................

j)  The door was so heavy that the child couldn't push it open.

The door was too ........................................................................................

3 **For questions a) – e),** *fill each of the gaps in the following sentences with* **one** *suitable word connected with* WEATHER CONDITIONS.

EXAMPLES: Police advised drivers to slow down because of the dense *fog*.

a) During the storm, the old tree was struck by ............................................... .

b) Just as we left for our picnic, the sun disappeared behind a large, grey
................................................. .

c) Lucy's doctor recommended that she should spend a few weeks in a
warmer ............................................... .

d) It was so ............................................... that my hat kept blowing off.

e) The weather forecast warned that there would be ten degrees of
............................................... overnight.

**For questions f) – j),** *the word in capitals below each of the following sentences can be used to form a word that fits suitably in the blank space. Fill each blank in this way.*

EXAMPLES: He said 'Good morning' in a most *friendly* way. FRIEND

My teacher *encouraged* me to take this examination. COURAGE

f) No-one with a recent ............................................... record will be considered for
this job. CRIME

g) We have decided to interview only the best six ............................................... for
the job. APPLY

h) David's ............................................... at winning the competition was clear to
everyone. ASTONISH

i) That large dog is perfectly ............................................... and has never been
known to attack anyone. HARM

j) Work is going on to ............................................... the bridge, which carries a
great deal of traffic. STRONG

4   *Make all the changes and additions necessary to produce, from the following sets of words and phrases, sentences which together make a complete letter. Note carefully from the example what kind of alterations need to be made. For each question, write a single sentence in the space provided.*

EXAMPLE:  I be very surprised / receive / letter / you this morning.

ANSWER:   *I was very surprised to receive a letter from you this morning.*

1 Willow Road
Cambridge CB3 2YN

1 September 1991

Dear Mrs Philips

I see / your advertisement / today's 'Cambridge News'.

a)   ...........................................................................................................................................

I like / apply / job / look / your two children / mornings.

b)   ...........................................................................................................................................

      ...........................................................................................................................................

At present, I be / student / local Technical College, / I study English part-time.

c)   ...........................................................................................................................................

      ...........................................................................................................................................

Although I be only twenty years old, I have / lot / experience / caring / children.

d)   ...........................................................................................................................................

      ...........................................................................................................................................

I have brothers /sisters younger / myself / last year I work / London / Mother's Help / ten months.

e)   ...........................................................................................................................................

      ...........................................................................................................................................

During / time, I be responsible / three-year-old boy / his mother be / work.

f) .............................................................................................................................

.............................................................................................................................

If you think I be suitable, please ring me / 72386 / we can arrange / time / meet.

g) .............................................................................................................................

.............................................................................................................................

The best time / call be / 6 pm, / I be always / home / that time.

h) .............................................................................................................................

.............................................................................................................................

I look forward / talk / you.

i) .............................................................................................................................

Yours sincerely

Antoinette Desmolines

5  *Lynford is a small, attractive town with a population of around 8,000. However, traffic in Lynford High Street, the only main road through the town, is becoming a problem. Local people realise something must be done to improve the situation and several have expressed their feelings in the local newspaper.*
*Look at the four proposals outlined below, together with the newspaper headlines and the information given on the map on page 72.*
*In your own words, complete the paragraphs on pages 72–3,* **using the information given** *and* **giving reasons for your choices.**

PROPOSAL 1:  Make Lynford High Street an express route. No stopping or parking allowed. Shop delivery vehicles only permitted between 9 pm and 6 am. Build two footbridges to allow pedestrians to cross the street.

PROPOSAL 2:  Build new road on west side of shops, crossing River Lyn. Close High Street to all traffic.

PROPOSAL 3:  Build tunnel to carry through traffic to Putchester. Limit High Street to local traffic and buses. Entrances to tunnel under Lynford to north and south of town.

PROPOSAL 4:  Introduce Park-and-Ride scheme. Provide free parking south of Lynford. Introduce cheap, regular service by bus or tram via High Street to Putchester.

RIVER LYN FLOODS AGAIN

BETTER PUBLIC TRANSPORT A NECESSITY

FOOTBRIDGES UNSUITABLE FOR DISABLED

LOCAL SHOPKEEPERS FEAR EXPRESS ROUTE

75% OF MOTORISTS AGAINST PARK-AND-RIDE SCHEME

"LET US FISH IN PEACE" SAY LOCALS

KEEP LYNFORD SAFE FOR SCHOOLCHILDREN

ROAD ACCIDENTS UP 10%

⟫⟶

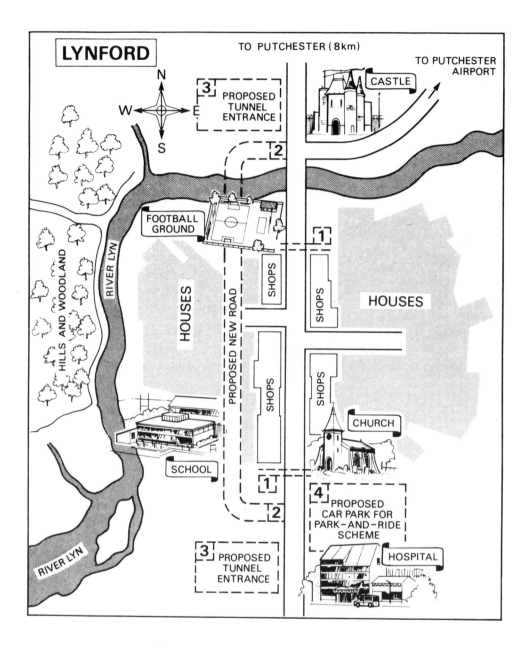

a) I think the best proposal would be to .................................................................

........................................................................................................................

........................................................................................................................

........................................................................................................................

........................................................................................................................................

........................................................................................................................................

........................................................................................................................................

........................................................................................................................................

b) Another good idea ............................................................................................................

........................................................................................................................................

........................................................................................................................................

........................................................................................................................................

........................................................................................................................................

........................................................................................................................................

........................................................................................................................................

c) However, I would reject the other two proposals for the following
reasons:

........................................................................................................................................

........................................................................................................................................

........................................................................................................................................

........................................................................................................................................

........................................................................................................................................

........................................................................................................................................

........................................................................................................................................

# PAPER 4  LISTENING COMPREHENSION
## (about 30 minutes)

**PART ONE**

*You will hear a woman talking about her life in London and comparing it with life in the country. Look at questions 1–6. Decide which of the statements are* TRUE *or* FALSE *and put a tick (√) in the appropriate box.*

|  | TRUE | FALSE |
|---|---|---|
| 1 She is thinking about leaving London. |  |  |
| 2 She never wanted to leave the country. |  |  |
| 3 She says that she goes out a lot. |  |  |
| 4 It would be easier to get to work if she had a car. |  |  |
| 5 She says that shopping is more convenient in London. |  |  |
| 6 She dislikes being so far from the country. |  |  |

**PART TWO**

*Look at the picture cards below. You are going to hear part of a game. In the game, a man describes one of the pictures on each of the cards.*
*For questions 7–11, tick (√) one of the boxes, A, B, C or D to show the correct answer. The first card is done for you as an example.*

CARD 1 (Example)

CARD 2

7

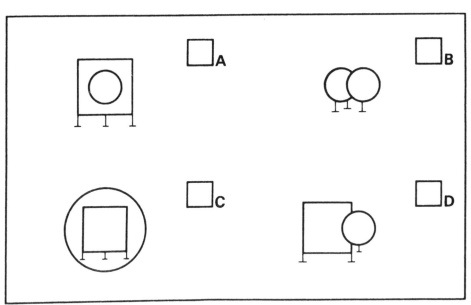

CARD 3

8

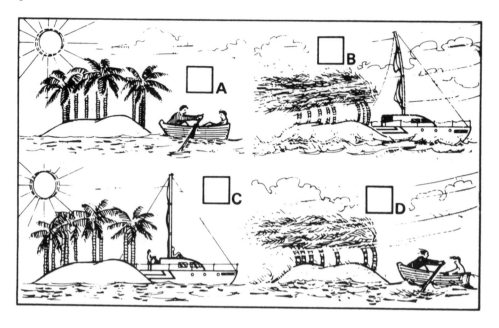

CARD 4

9

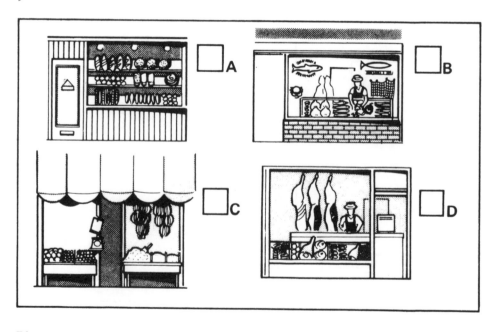

CARD 5

10

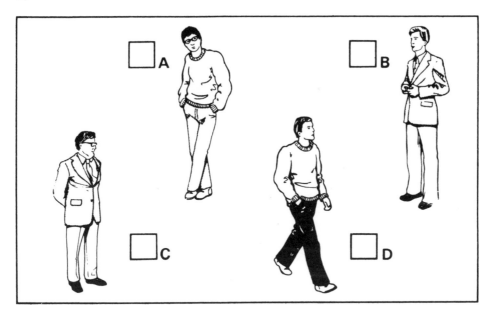

CARD 6

11

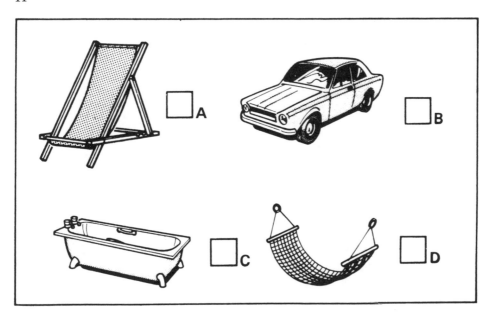

## PART THREE

*You will hear a conversation between two women. Lisa is telling her friend, Janet, what happened to her when she went for an interview.*
*For questions 12–15, tick (√) one of the boxes A, B, C or D to show the correct answer.*

12  How would you describe Lisa's day?

| | |
|---|---|
| A exciting | A |
| B annoying | B |
| C boring | C |
| D sad | D |

13  How does Janet react to Lisa's story? She is

| | |
|---|---|
| A sympathetic | A |
| B amazed | B |
| C upset | C |
| D amused | D |

14  How does Lisa feel about the way the railway company arranged for her to get home?

| | |
|---|---|
| A grateful | A |
| B angry | B |
| C relieved | C |
| D critical | D |

15  Which one of these pictures best describes Lisa's return journey? Tick (√) the correct box.

| | |
|---|---|
| A | |
| B | |
| C | |
| D | |

A

B

C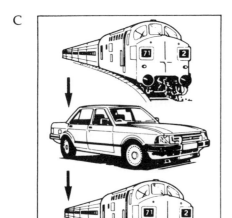

D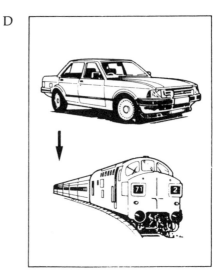

## PART FOUR

*You will hear a secretary talking to her boss about plans for the next two weeks.*
*For questions 16–24, fill in the spaces in the office diary using a few words.*

| *April* | *April* |
|---|---|
| 12 MON **No Appointments** | 19 MON [20] |
| 13 TUE [16] [17] | 20 TUE *No Appointments* [21] |
| 14 WED [18] *(may take all day)* | 21 WED *No Appointments* [22] |
| 15 THU *Regular monthly head office meeting* | 22 THU *No Appointments* [23] |
| 16 FRI *Probably in* [19] | 23 FRI *Probably going to* [24] |
| 17 SAT 18 SUN ////////// | 24 SAT 25 SUN ////////// |

## PAPER 5   INTERVIEW   (about 15 minutes)

You will be asked to take part in a theme-directed conversation with the examiner. You may be by yourself, with another candidate or with two other candidates. (Two examiners are present when there are three candidates.) The conversation will be based on one particular topic area, for example holidays, work, food.

A typical interview is described below.

★ You will be shown one, two or three photographs and invited to talk about them.

★ The examiner will then show you one or more passages and invite you to link them to the theme. You may be asked to talk a little about the content of the passage. You will *not*, however, be asked to read the passage aloud but you may quote parts of it to make your point.

★ You will then be asked to take part in a communicative activity with the other candidates present and/or the examiner (or examiners). This could involve role-play, problem solving, planning, rank ordering etc. or it could be a discussion on another aspect of the general theme of the conversation. Advertisements, diagrams and other realia are often used as stimuli here.

You will find six sample First Certificate interviews at the back of this book. Your teacher can help you to prepare for this part of the examination by assuming the role of the examiner and telling you which item in the Interview Exercises you should look at.

# Practice Test 5

## PAPER 1   READING COMPREHENSION   (1 hour)

*Answer all questions. Indicate your choice of answer in every case* **on the separate answer sheet** *already given out, which should show your name and examination index number. Follow carefully the instructions about how to record your answers. Give* **one answer only** *to each question. Marks will not be deducted for wrong answers: your total score on this test will be the number of correct answers you give.*

### SECTION A

*In this section you must choose the word or phrase which best completes each sentence.* **On your answer sheet** *indicate the letter A, B, C or D against the number of each item 1 to 25 for the word or phrase you choose.*

1   The newspaper report contained ................ important information.
   A many   B another   C an   D a lot of

2   She refused to eat meat under any ................ .
   A circumstances   B occasion   C opportunity   D reason

3   I left my last job because I had no ................ to travel.
   A place   B position   C opportunity   D possibility

4   The meeting had to be put ................ until a later date.
   A away   B on   C off   D up

5   He had to leave early, ................ he?
   A didn't   B mustn't   C hasn't   D shouldn't

6   He missed the lecture, so I lent him my notes ................ .
   A after   B afterwards   C at last   D finally

7   If only he ................ accept some help with the work instead of trying to do it alone!
   A will   B may   C would   D were

8   I'll show you around the city, when you ................ to visit me.
   A come   B are coming   C will come   D will be coming

9  That ................. table used to belong to my great grandmother.
   A aged      B mature      C elderly      D antique

10  These buses are ................. to run every 15 minutes, but I've been waiting here
   for 25 minutes already.
   A assumed      B promised      C presumed      D supposed

11  His eyes were ................. bad that he couldn't read the number plate of the car
   in front.
   A such      B too      C so      D very

12  The poor child was in floods of ................. because his bicycle had been stolen.
   A weeping      B crying      C tears      D unhappiness

13  She kindly offered to ................. me the way to the station.
   A explain      B direct      C describe      D show

14  She can remember a time ................. cars were rarely seen in the village.
   A which      B that      C where      D when

15  I can't find my dictionary at the moment. I hope it will ................. up soon.
   A come      B clear      C turn      D look

16  The window was so high up, that ................. you could see was the sky.
   A everything      B all      C only      D just

17  We have bought extra food ................. our friends stay to dinner.
   A in case      B if      C provided      D as long as

18  He likes to take ................. in sport, not only to watch it.
   A practice      B place      C exercise      D part

19  The police have warned tourists to look ................. for pickpockets in the town
   centre.
   A up      B down      C forward      D out

20  The children ................. at the beautiful picture with a sense of wonder.
   A gazed      B admired      C glared      D glanced

21  I wouldn't ................. of going to a party I hadn't been invited to.
   A intend      B dream      C rely      D depend

22  If you want to be healthy, you should cut ................. on your smoking.
   A down      B up      C through      D out

23  I hope we will be able to avoid ................. anyone.
    A disappointment    B disappointing    C disappointed
    D disappoint

24  He was clearly nervous; he was sitting right on the ................. of his chair.
    A outside    B edge    C tip    D border

25  There were over 30,000 ................. at the match.
    A spectators    B viewers    C witnesses    D watchers

## SECTION B

*In this section you will find after each of the passages a number of questions or
unfinished statements about the passage, each with four suggested answers or ways of
finishing. You must choose the one which you think fits best according to the passage.*
**On your answer sheet,** *indicate the letter A, B, C or D against the number of each
item* **26–40** *for the answer you choose. Give* **one answer only** *to each question. Read
each passage right through before choosing your answers.*

### FIRST PASSAGE

I climbed downwards towards some trees giving some shelter, where I could
rest for a few minutes and watch the sea. It was then that I saw the boat. It was
tied up close to a small inlet where the land curved and the water was
comparatively smooth. There was no mistaking the boat; it was theirs all right.
The Greek they employed as crew was seated in the bows, with a fishing line
over the side, but from his relaxed attitude the fishing did not seem to be
serious, and I judged he was having a sleep. He was the only occupant of the
boat. I glanced directly beneath me at the sand along the shore, and I saw there
was a rough stone building, more or less ruined, built against the cliff-face,
possibly used at one time as a shelter for sheep or goats. There was a big bag
and a picnic basket lying by the entrance, and a coat. Mr and Mrs Stoll must
have landed earlier from the boat and were now resting.
　　Suddenly the person in the boat sat up, and winding in his line he moved
to the back and stood there, watching the water. I saw something move, a form
beneath the surface, and then the form itself emerged. Then it was hidden from
me by the Greek bending to assist the swimmer, and my attention was diverted
to the ruined shelter on the shore. Something was standing in the entrance. I
say 'something' because, doubtless because of a trick of the light, it had at first
the hairy appearance of a horse standing on its back legs. Legs and back were
covered with hair, and then I realised it was Stoll himself, naked, his arms and
chest as hairy as the rest of him. Only his swollen red face showed what he was,
with the enormous ears like saucers standing out either side of his bald head. I

had never before in all my life seen a more horrible sight. He came out into the sunlight and looked towards the boat, and then, as if well pleased with himself and his world, walked forward, up and down the beach before the ruined shelter with that curious movement I had noticed earlier in the village.

The swimmer was now coming into the beach with long leisurely strokes. When she reached the shore and stood up, I saw, with astonishment, that it was Mrs Stoll. She was carrying some kind of bag around her neck, and advancing up the sand to meet her husband she lifted it over her head and gave it to him. I did not hear them exchange a word, and they went together to the hut and disappeared inside.

26  The writer was heading towards the trees because he
    A  wanted to watch a boat on the sea.
    B  wanted no-one to see him.
    C  wanted to spy on the people below.
    D  wanted to find somewhere to sit.

27  When the writer looked below him, he saw
    A  some people having a picnic.
    B  the Greek man asleep on the beach.
    C  some sheep and some goats.
    D  some of the Stolls' possessions.

28  Why did the person in the boat move to the back?
    A  Because he had seen something move there.
    B  Because he was going to help somebody.
    C  Because he had seen some fish.
    D  Because he had left his fishing line there.

29  When the writer looked at the shelter again, he saw
    A  someone he recognised.
    B  an animal like a horse.
    C  someone walking towards the boat.
    D  something coming out of the sea.

30  What did Mrs Stoll do when she got out of the water?
    A  She took something out of the bag.
    B  She went straight to the hut.
    C  She gave something to her husband.
    D  She put the bag down on the sand.

SECOND PASSAGE

It is not difficult for me to guess why I developed a love of cats in my life. Cats will let us love them, in fact they plainly wish us to, but they will not love us in return, though many of us persuade ourselves that they do. On the other hand, they do not pretend to return our feelings, nor do they make promises that they cannot or will not keep.

I never saw my cat Tim hurry; nobody did, even when he was catching mice, though long before he died he had given up trying to do so. It was not that he was a lazy cat; I think he had come to the conclusion that the mice had just as much right to live as he had, and since they were not his enemies and he would have disliked eating one, he could see no point in stretching out a soft paw to bring it down on a struggling back.

He was proud but gentle; I remember as a child putting my finger to his mouth to feel his warm breath, and despite the fact that he normally avoided showing affection, he licked my finger slowly, so that I felt for the first time that curious roughness that all cats' tongues have.

He would never play in the ordinary sense; a ball on the end of a string he ignored, and though he would occasionally go after one rolled across the floor he would not, having caught it, repeat the action as soon as he realised it was only a game. Nor would he ever beg; it was beneath his dignity, and besides, his wants were few.

Tim was the only cat I have ever known who understood what a mirror was. In my grandfather's shop there was a full-length mirror, too big and heavy to hang or even fix, so it stood against the wall with its base a few inches out. All other cats I have ever seen before a mirror were confused; they either failed to see their reflection or, seeing it, would think it was another cat, and, after putting out an exploratory paw, would run around behind the mirror, into the space made by the angle at which it leaned against the wall. Tim was plainly aware that it was his own self that he saw in it – but he did not need the mirror to tell him he was handsome; it is generally only the man or woman who lacks confidence who needs constantly to look in the mirror, and doubtless the same applies to cats.

31  The writer loves cats because they do not
    A  deceive us about their feelings.
    B  care whether we love them.
    C  need much human company.
    D  need much looking after.

32  The writer's cat stopped catching mice because he
    A  was too old to run.
    B  had other enemies.
    C  always had enough to eat.
    D  felt it was unfair.

33  Why would the writer's cat chase a ball only once?
    A  He refused to play games.
    B  He realised he could not eat it.
    C  He preferred playing with other things.
    D  He could not catch it.

34  The writer says that when most cats look in a mirror they
    A  understand that they are looking at themselves.
    B  enjoy looking at themselves.
    C  think there is another cat behind it.
    D  hide behind it because they are afraid.

35  The writer's cat didn't look in the mirror because he
    A  had seen his reflection many times.
    B  did not like looking at his reflection.
    C  lacked confidence.
    D  was content with his appearance.

THIRD PASSAGE

Mark Boxer was entirely self-taught and strongly opposed to any form of art training, which he thought had the effect of weakening any natural, individual ability. His own ability (he wasn't vain about it, though he knew he was good) meant a great struggle in pursuit of perfection. He always refused to draw people he didn't know or hadn't met. Watching them on video might be good enough: a glance, the shape of an eyebrow, a wave of the hand all helped. Sometimes he took a table in a restaurant if he knew his subject would be there. He'd ask to see people at their office and walk around them while they made telephone calls or ran meetings.

If he was asked to draw someone who didn't interest him, he'd ask if a photograph could be used instead. He never understood how he could be expected to draw someone for whom he had no feeling, whose face or character didn't make him want to draw them. There were certain people he could not draw. Ordinary, good-looking faces didn't interest him, and he found women difficult. There were also certain people whom, out of a sense of decency, he refused to make fun of with his drawing.

Most of his drawings were done to accompany the weekly column in a Sunday newspaper. If the drawing went well he'd have the outline of it by eight o'clock on Thursday evening, and enjoy his supper. He then went on until late. There was a lot of walking up and down and hurried searching through reference books and piles of photographs. Dozens of unfinished drawings ended up in the waste-paper basket. If it didn't come right, he'd give up, look unhappy and tired, and get ready for bed. On Friday morning he would phone the paper and tell them it was no good. When he was drawing, the lines were always quick and confident. He started with pencil and ended up with an old-fashioned pen. He took great pleasure in colouring or inking in parts of a drawing which made the old pens scatter ink everywhere. The floor in his study is still covered with black ink spots from pens shaken to get just the right amount of ink.

He sat on a high stool, pen in mouth, a number of pens or pencils in his right hand as he drew with his left. Some years ago, while playing cricket (his favourite game), he made a great jump for a catch and broke his thumb. Badly set, it looked awkward, but he swore he drew better afterwards, with a more economical line.

36  What do we learn about Mark Boxer and art training?
 A  He was glad he hadn't had any.
 B  He thought he was too good to need it.
 C  It didn't influence the way he drew.
 D  It had improved his technique.

37  He would only agree to draw someone if
 A  he could meet them.
 B  they appealed to him.
 C  he had a photograph of them.
 D  they were well known.

38  If Mark was happy with his drawings for the Sunday paper
 A  he would work into the night.
 B  he would finish work before supper.
 C  he wouldn't need to use his reference books.
 D  he would telephone the office.

39  Why were there black ink spots on his floor?
 A  The pens leaked because they were old.
 B  The pens sometimes fell on the floor.
 C  He spilt ink when filling the pens.
 D  He shook ink off the pens.

40  What do we learn about Mark and his work?
 A  He thought he was perfect.
 B  He had very high standards.
 C  He had to struggle to complete anything.
 D  He could draw anything if he tried.

# PAPER 2   COMPOSITION   (1½ hours)

*Write **two only** of the following composition exercises. Your answers must follow exactly the instructions given and must be of between 120 and 180 words each.*

1   You have recently discovered the address of a friend whom you haven't seen for five years. Write a letter telling him/her about the changes in your life and suggesting a meeting.

2   A new road is being planned which could cut through the only park in your neighbourhood. You attend a public meeting to protest against this plan. Write what you say.

3   Write a description of someone you admire and respect, either someone you know or a famous person.

4   'Some jobs are more suitable for men and others are more suitable for women.' Do you think this is still true?

5   Based on your reading of *one* of these books, write on **one** of the following.

   MAYA ANGELOU: *I Know Why the Caged Bird Sings*
   Describe two events which greatly affected Maya as a child. What effect do you think they had on her character?

   LAURIE LEE: *Cider with Rosie*
   Describe Laurie's life in the infant school and how it changed when he entered 'THE BIG ROOM'.

   H. G. WELLS: *The Invisible Man*
   'He is mad,' said Kemp, 'inhuman.' Why did Dr Kemp say this about the Invisible Man? Do you agree with him?

# PAPER 3   USE OF ENGLISH   (2 hours)

1   *Fill each of the numbered blanks in the following passage. Use only* **one** *word in each space.*

Last Wednesday, Mary went to a concert with her friend Julia. The concert-hall was on the other side of the town and so they decided to (1) .............................. home early. They caught the bus and arrived long (2) .............................. the concert was due to start. There was a cafe nearby so they went in. Mary ordered a sandwich and coffee but Julia decided to have a hot meal. While they were waiting to (3) .............................. served, Mary looked (4) .............................. her handbag for the tickets to check what time the concert (5) .............................. begin.

To (6) .............................. dismay, she discovered that the tickets were not there! Then she remembered that she (7) .............................. left them on the table at home. She told Julia (8) .............................. had happened and said she would go home to get the tickets. She promised to be (9) .............................. before the concert started.

Mary rushed (10) .............................. of the cafe and went to the bus-stop to catch a bus back to her house. Unfortunately, she had just (11) .............................. a bus and she (12) .............................. to wait a long time for (13) .............................. one. She was just beginning to despair (14) .............................. she saw a taxi, which she signalled to stop. Giving her address to the driver, she jumped (15) .............................. , and fifteen minutes later she was home. 'Wait for me,' she said and ran into the house. Mary picked (16) .............................. the tickets from the table and the taxi-driver drove her straight back to the cafe.

Julia had just finished her meal. Together they hurried out of the cafe and walked quickly to the concert-hall, (17) .............................. they arrived hot and (18) .............................. of breath. Mary showed the tickets to the man at the door, (19) .............................. looked at them carefully and then (20) .............................. them back. 'I'm sorry,' he said. 'These are for next Wednesday.'

2   *Finish each of the following sentences in such a way that it means the same as the sentence printed before it.*

EXAMPLE:  I haven't enjoyed myself so much for years.

ANSWER:   It's years *since I enjoyed myself so much.*

a)  If you don't want Sally to be angry with you, I suggest you apologise.
    You'd .........................................................................................................................
    .........................................................................................................................

b)  You might fall if you're not careful.
    Be careful .................................................................................................................

c)  Mrs Edwards is the owner of that car.
    That car ....................................................................................................................

d)  The station clock showed half-past ten.
    According ..................................................................................................................

e)  Henry found a wallet with no name in it.
    The wallet ..................................................................................................................

f)  Ronald denied stealing Mrs Clark's handbag.
    Ronald said that .........................................................................................................

g)  Susan likes staying in hotels but she prefers camping.
    Susan doesn't .............................................................................................................
    .........................................................................................................................

h)  The fridge was so heavy that we couldn't move it.
    The fridge was too ......................................................................................................

i)  'John, please don't tell anyone my new address,' said Mary.
    Mary asked .................................................................................................................

j)   The judges had never seen a prettier flower display.

It was ...................................................................................................................................

3   **For questions a) – e),** *fill each of the gaps in the following sentences with* **one** *suitable word connected with* BUYING AND SELLING.

EXAMPLE:  Keep the *receipt* for this shirt in case it doesn't fit you.

a)   My watch was a real ............................................... . It is worth three times the price I paid for it.

b)   'I'm afraid we don't have any more of those computers in

............................................... , Madam,' said the sales assistant.

c)   That department store is offering a 10% ............................................... to customers who spend more than £100 today.

d)   Ice-cream and chocolate were on ............................................... during the interval.

e)   'The radio I bought here this morning doesn't work properly, so I would

like to ............................................... it for another one,' said Elizabeth.

**For questions f) – j),** *the word in capitals below each of the following sentences can be used to form a word that fits suitably in the blank space. Fill each blank in this way.*

EXAMPLES:  He said 'Good morning' in a most *friendly* way.     FRIEND

My teacher *encouraged* me to take this examination.   COURAGE

f)   The crowd showed its ............................................... by shouting insults at the players.                                         APPROVE

g)   Dozens of ............................................... are injured on the city's roads each year.

CYCLE

h)   The company is not taking on any new ............................................... this year.

EMPLOY

i)   Carl is studying to become a ............................................... .       LAW

j)   Motor-racing is an extremely ............................................... sport.       RISK

4 *Make all the changes and additions necessary to produce, from the following sets of words and phrases, sentences which together make a complete letter. Note carefully from the example what kind of alterations need to be made. For each question, write a single sentence in the space provided.*

EXAMPLE: I be very surprised / receive / letter / you this morning.

ANSWER: *I was very surprised to receive a letter from you this morning.*

> 12 Lindsay Street
> Manchester M14 6EJ
>
> 2 June 1991

Dear Carol

Thank you very much / invitation / spend three weeks / August / you / your family / Scotland.

a) ................................................................................................................

................................................................................................................

I love / come / unfortunately I be unable / accept.

b) ................................................................................................................

................................................................................................................

My cousins, / live / Canada, / stay / us / August 3rd / August 18th.

c) ................................................................................................................

................................................................................................................

As it be / first visit / this country, I plan / show them around.

d) ................................................................................................................

................................................................................................................

It be possible / visit you / September instead?

e) ................................................................................................................

................................................................................................................

I certainly need / rest after / cousins go back / Canada!

f) ................................................................................................................

Please tell / September be convenient.

g) ........................................................................................................................................

   I look forward / see you all again.

h) ........................................................................................................................................

   ........................................................................................................................................

   Love

   Cordelia

5   *The TV programme 'Travel Bug' is holding a competition in which viewers can win **one** of the holidays advertised below. The viewers have to state which of the holidays would be best for them and why.*

*Below are the entry coupons of three viewers:*

| NAME Harris | FIRST NAME Ada | |
|---|---|---|
| STATUS Widow | AGE 65 | PROFESSION Retired Headmistress |
| INTERESTS Sight-seeing, novels, painting | | |

| NAME Dixon | FIRST NAME Carol | |
|---|---|---|
| STATUS Single | AGE 24 | PROFESSION Nurse |
| INTERESTS Outdoor Sports, Photography | | |

| NAME Rippon | FIRST NAME Tina | |
|---|---|---|
| STATUS Married | AGE 36 | PROFESSION Housewife |
| INTERESTS Cooking, dancing, yoga, looking after my two young children. | | |

**Using the information given,** *complete the paragraphs on page 96. In your own* words, **explain and give reasons** *why each entrant has made her particular choice.*

≫→

a) I think that Ada .......................................................................................................................

.......................................................................................................................

.......................................................................................................................

.......................................................................................................................

.......................................................................................................................

.......................................................................................................................

.......................................................................................................................

b) On the other hand, Carol ...........................................................................................

.......................................................................................................................

.......................................................................................................................

.......................................................................................................................

.......................................................................................................................

.......................................................................................................................

.......................................................................................................................

c) I expect that Tina .........................................................................................................

.......................................................................................................................

.......................................................................................................................

.......................................................................................................................

.......................................................................................................................

.......................................................................................................................

.......................................................................................................................

# PAPER 4   LISTENING COMPREHENSION
## (about 30 minutes)

### PART ONE

*You will hear Robert talking to his parents about an adventure holiday.*
*For questions 1–8, answer the questions with a word or a short phrase.*

1  How old is Robert's friend, John?

| 1 | |
|---|---|

2  Where did Robert and his family stay when on holiday last year?

| 2 | |
|---|---|

3  What sort of holiday does Robert's father suggest?

| 3 | |
|---|---|

4  Who enjoys playing on a beach?

| 4 | |
|---|---|

5  Name one thing that worries Robert's mother.

| 5 | |
|---|---|

Name three activities apart from sailing and climbing that people can do at the adventure centre Robert is interested in.

| 6 | |
|---|---|

| 7 | |
|---|---|

| 8 | |
|---|---|

## PART TWO

*You will hear a British woman describing a holiday she had in Moscow.*
*Look at questions 9–16. Which of the statements are* TRUE, *which are* FALSE *and*
*which are* NOT STATED *by the speaker?*
*Indicate the right answer by* (circling) *as in the examples.*

| | |
|---|---|
| EXAMPLE: She took an afternoon flight. | TRUE/FALSE/NOT STATED |
| EXAMPLE: She flew British Airways. | TRUE/FALSE/NOT STATED |

9  The weather was warmer than the speaker
   had expected.                                     TRUE/FALSE/NOT STATED

10  The speaker found that the time difference
     affected her.                                        TRUE/FALSE/NOT STATED

11  They had plenty of time to plan their
     entertainment programme.                       TRUE/FALSE/NOT STATED

12  The underground stations are a long way
     below street level.                               TRUE/FALSE/NOT STATED

13  There were colourful advertisements on
     the streets.                                    TRUE/FALSE/NOT STATED

14  They found it difficult to understand
     people's directions.                             TRUE/FALSE/NOT STATED

15  There was a shortage of milk and eggs in
     the shops.                                    TRUE/FALSE/NOT STATED

16  The speaker bought a lot of presents for
     friends at home.                                 TRUE/FALSE/NOT STATED

## PART THREE

*You will hear part of a radio interview with Laura Kassinada, who is a member of an*
*organisation called the International Alliance of Women. Laura tells the interviewer*
*about the alliance and particularly its work in India.*
*For questions 17–20, tick (√) one of the boxes A, B, C or D to show the correct answer.*

17  One aim of the project was to help women to

   A  do their housework.

   B  help others living nearby.

   C  work in local industries.

   D  learn how to sew.

| A | |
|---|---|
| B | |
| C | |
| D | |

18  What have women in the project been taught to do or make?

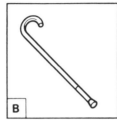
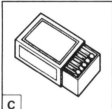

| A | |
|---|---|
| B | |
| C | |
| D | |

19  Which picture shows the most likely carpentry group?

| A | |
|---|---|
| B | |
| C | |
| D | |

20  What are the women encouraged to do with the things they make?

A  to sell them independently

B  to sell them in their houses

C  to give them to other people to sell

D  to keep all the things they make

| | |
|---|---|
| A | |
| B | |
| C | |
| D | |

## PART FOUR

*You will hear a conversation between a young couple, Kari and David. They are going to visit some relatives, whom they have never met, and they are discussing what sort of presents to take with them for the family.*
*For questions 21–25, write what they have decided to take next to each name.*

Uncle Robert     21

Auntie Val      22

Jasper        23

Natalie       24

Freddie       25

# PAPER 5   INTERVIEW   (about 15 minutes)

You will be asked to take part in a theme-directed conversation with the examiner. You may be by yourself, with another candidate or with two other candidates. (Two examiners are present when there are three candidates.) The conversation will be based on one particular topic area, for example holidays, work, food.

A typical interview is described below.

★ You will be shown one, two or three photographs and invited to talk about them.

★ The examiner will then show you one or more passages and invite you to link them to the theme. You may be asked to talk a little about the content of the passage. You will *not*, however, be asked to read the passage aloud but you may quote parts of it to make your point.

★ You will then be asked to take part in a communicative activity with the other candidates present and/or the examiner (or examiners). This could involve role-play, problem solving, planning, rank ordering etc. or it could be a discussion on another aspect of the general theme of the conversation. Advertisements, diagrams and other realia are often used as stimuli here.

You will find six sample First Certificate interviews at the back of this book. Your teacher can help you to prepare for this part of the examination by assuming the role of the examiner and telling you which item in the Interview Exercises you should look at.

# Interview Exercises

## PRACTICE TEST 1

### TRAVEL AND HOLIDAYS

1

**2**

**3**

**4**  Motorists should remember that young children and animals should never be left unattended in an unventilated car in hot weather. It is essential that all windows should be left open at least one inch in excessive heat and a supply of cool drinks should be constantly available. Regular stops for fresh air and exercise are also strongly recommended.

**5**  Having a great time in spite of the weather! It's poured with rain every day since we arrived, and knowing you're all enjoying a heat-wave at home doesn't help! However, it's great fun and the kids are loving the adventure of sleeping and eating in a tent!

**6**  Swimming pools in Tokyo flowed to capacity yesterday as thousands of families took a day's holiday to escape the summer heat. About 30,000 people visited Korakuen amusement park and there was standing-room only in the huge swimming pool.

**7**  *Choosing a Holiday*

| | | |
|---|---|---|
| weather | cost | opportunities to meet people |
| scenery | food | comfort |
| entertainment | relaxation | places to visit |

**8**  (i) My annual holiday is the high spot of my year.

(ii) I'd rather have a new car or buy something else I've always wanted than have a holiday.

(i) 'Holidays at home are not real holidays.'

(ii) A holiday is all very well, but there is no place like home.

**9**

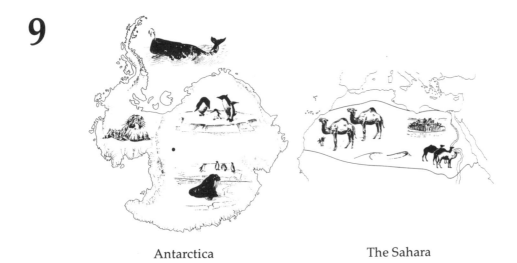

Antarctica                    The Sahara

## PRACTICE TEST 2

### FASHION AND CLOTHES

**10**

**11**

**12**

**13** The bride wore a full-length white gown made of silk. She wore a veil with a headdress, and carried a bouquet of roses. The groom was in military uniform. After a reception at the Viking Hotel, York, the couple left for a honeymoon in Paris.

**14** *Don't be a shrinking violet!* The message for this season is clear. *Stand tall and be seen!* Colours are bold and hats should be big and exciting. Our model is wearing a flame red poppy hat which is shown to dramatic effect by the simple black dress and long black gloves.

**15** I wear what I like and I couldn't care less what other people think. I choose practical things that I feel comfortable in. A lot of people say I look like Harry, my boyfriend, but I don't think it's deliberate, it just happens that way.

**16**

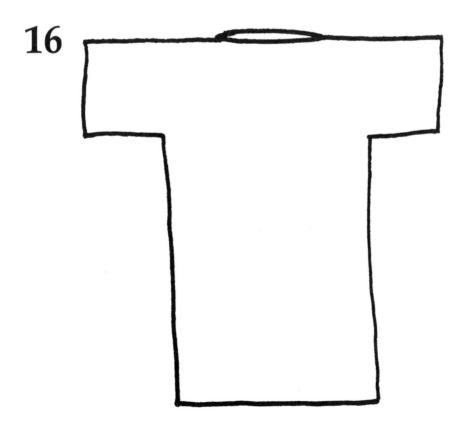

**17** *Events*

discotheque     beach party     sight-seeing trip
wedding         formal dinner     tennis match with friends
barbecue       theatre          funeral

**18** *'Fashion is only for women.'*

## PRACTICE TEST 3

### NEIGHBOURS AND NEIGHBOURHOODS

**19**

**20**

**21**

**22** Of course it's impersonal but that's what I like. I couldn't wait to get away from home where everyone knew everything about everyone. Here, life is much more civilised. The apartments in my block are small but neat. They're all burglar-proof and we all have our own key for the elevator. My office is only a few blocks away and there are plenty of clubs, cinemas, theatres etc. nearby. It's really great!

**23** The picturesque town of Richmond is situated in Swaledale, North Yorkshire. It is a sleepy little town dominated by the ruins of its ancient castle, with narrow, winding streets leading down to the river, so loved by artists. Although it is a busy market town, much of its village atmosphere still remains. Here, life is peaceful, calm and quiet.

**24** Everyone in the village works together for the good of the community. They lead a simple life but everyone has his or her role to play. Often, when the work is done and while the children are playing, the men sit and chat together. The women sing as they prepare the food in a communal hut.

**25** 'East, west, home's best.'
'Home is where the heart is.'
'The other man's grass is always greener.'

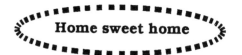

**26** *Building Plans*

| | |
|---|---|
| sports centre | cinema and theatre |
| shopping centre | park with children's playground |
| office block | multi-storey car park |

**27** *Neighbours*
1  an elderly woman with four cats
2  a young couple with three children
3  a retired couple
4  a single woman who teaches dancing
5  two students with motorbikes
6  a professional couple with a dog

## PRACTICE TEST 4

### HAVING A GOOD TIME

**28**

**29**

**30**

**31** It's just getting so expensive – sometimes a ride costs £1 and the drinks and the food cost three times as much as in town. Mind you, the kids have a wonderful time so I shouldn't grumble.

**32**  Crisps are my favourite but I like sausages on sticks as well.
Afterwards we play games and sometimes I win a prize.

**33**  Dear Magda

Still enjoying it here – wish you could have stayed till the end
of term, we had a great celebration, which started in the classroom!
I haven't decided what to do when I get back but perhaps I should
stay with the family for a few weeks.

See you soon,

*Kate.*

**34**

| HAVING A GOOD TIME | |
|---|---|
| – Dancing | – Parties |
| – Eating out | – Theatre |
| – Walking in the country | – Shopping |
| – Playing games | – Lying on the beach |
| – Reading | – Sports |

**35**

Holidays are great and worth every penny.

Holidays are a waste of time and money.

Lying in the sun is dangerous.

Holidays are boring unless there are lots of things to do.

Sightseeing is not worth the effort.

All work and no play makes Jack a dull boy.

Families always quarrel on holiday.

**36** You have just finished all your examinations and have done very well. You are arranging a celebration with your friend(s). Decide what you would like to do and make the necessary arrangements.

*Possible activities*

A party at your house
An evening in a disco
A trip to the theatre / cinema
A picnic
A meal in a restaurant
Balloon trip! / Windsurfing day! / Mountain expedition!
Other suggestions . . .

## PRACTICE TEST 5

### CHILDHOOD

**37**

**38**

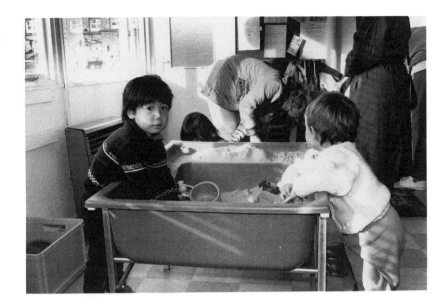

**39**

**40** I started when I was only five – it seemed easy because my piano teacher made practising feel like a game and I always got a reward for playing something new properly. It's different now, of course. . . .

**41** School uniform and the wearing of school colours to be strongly encouraged.
*Girls*: Bottle-green cardigan or jumper, green skirt, white blouse. School tie may be worn.
*Boys*: Bottle-green jumper, grey or white shirt, grey shorts or trousers, school tie.

**42** HELP! Our play-group is getting bigger and bigger but we need more people to look after the children and some more toys, especially for the four-year-olds. Please contact Sarah on 587-2432 if you can help.

**43**

# Activity English

## VARESTOY CAMP, NORTH WALES

*Learn English by the sea!*

The camp offers many sports facilities:

● Canoeing, swimming, diving, tennis, mountain climbing and horse-riding.

● Lots of activities and entertainment.

● Lessons available in English every day.

● TENTS or small CABINS in the forest.

● Open ALL year.

● Children aged from 10–16. Parents or older relatives welcome as helpers.

*For more information and details*
Telephone: Mary Davies   235-231

# 44

*Bluebird*
**A LA CART KITCHEN**
Every child's dream kitchen for
hours of fun, with
many accessories.
Ages 3-up.
£**25**.87

*Tonka*
**TINY TEARS**
14" crying, wetting
doll with nappy, bottle
and dummy.
Ages 3-up.
£**12**.87 Each

*Texas Instruments*
**SPEAK AND SPELL**
150 word vocabulary, range of
games and activities.
Ages 6-11.
(Batteries sold separately)
£**29**.87

*Little Tikes*
**COZY COUPE**
Opening door, horn,
storage compartment.
Ages 1½-5.
£**39**.87

# 45  'Cities are terrible places for children to grow up in.'

## OPTIONAL READING

**LAURIE LEE:** *Cider with Rosie*

# 46

**47**

**48**

**49** The cottage stood in a large garden on a steep slope above a lake. It had rooms on three floors as well as a cellar; it had a pump to bring up water from a well; and apple trees, great masses of flowers and fruit bushes; and birds in the chimney, frogs in the cellar, things growing on damp ceilings; all for a rent of three shillings and sixpence a week.

**50**    This man did not look like a soldier. He had no polished brass, no leather belt, no waxed moustaches like my uncles. He had a beard, and his khaki was torn. But the girls were sure that he was a soldier, and said it in whispers, like a secret.

**51**    Then there was Willy-the-Fish, who came round from house to house on Fridays, selling fish that was so old that even my family couldn't eat it. Willy was a loose-lipped, sad-eyed man who had lost his girl because of his trade. He used to lean by our door, and blow and scratch, and tell us the sad story of how he'd lost her.

**52**    But even today, when the sky darkens suddenly, and a storm builds up in the west, and I smell rain in the wind and hear the first sound of distant thunder, then I grow uneasy, and start looking for brooms.

**53**    'Come and help me, someone!' Crabby shouted madly. But nobody moved; we just watched. We saw Spadge lift her and place her on the top of the cupboard, then walk out of the door and away from the school. There was a moment of silence, then we all put down our pens and began to drum steadily on the floor with our feet.

**54**    Dorothy was as quick-moving as a wildcat, attractive, and very noisy. And she protected us boys with fire and spirit, and brought us treasures from the outside world. When I think of her now, she is a twist of smoke, a giggling spitting fire, a smell of gunpowder.

**55**    In serving out food, Mother had no method, and even the laws of chance didn't work – a dab on each plate in any order, and then it was a race. There was no thanksgiving, no warning, no starting-gun; the first one to finish what had been on his plate could claim what was left in the pot.

**56**  When darkness fell, and the great moon rose, we began a second life. Then boys went calling along the roads, wild narrow-eyed animal calls. As soon as we heard them, we crept out of doors, out of our airless bedrooms, into moonlight as warm as the sun, to join our chalk-white, moon-changed group.

**57**  Now I was free to become one of the audience; the Entertainment was mine, and I was there to enjoy it. Mr Crosby, the organist, told jokes and stories as if his life depended on them. He trembled and sweated, never pausing for a laugh.

**58**  Close under the yew trees, in the heavy green evening, we sat solemnly down. The old red yews threw arches above us. In the rusty darkness, Jo, like a small straight yew branch, was quite still; she neither looked at me nor away. I threw a stone into the trees, heard it falling from branch to branch.

**59**

ENTER CANDIDATE
NUMBER HERE →

NOW SHOW THE
NUMBER BY
MARKING THE GRID

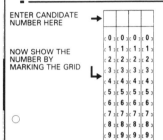

Examination/Paper No.

Examination Title

Centre No.

ENTER CANDIDATE NAME HERE:

........................................................

- Tell the Invigilator immediately if the
  information above is not correct.

## MULTIPLE-CHOICE ANSWER SHEET

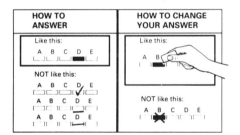

HOW TO
ANSWER

Like this:
A B C D E

NOT like this:
A B C D E
A B C D E
A B C D E

HOW TO CHANGE
YOUR ANSWER

Like this:
A B

NOT like this:
A B C D E

**DO**
- use an HB pencil
- rub out any answer
  you wish to change

**DON'T**
- use any other kind of pen
  or pencil
- use correcting fluid
- make any marks outside
  the boxes

| 1 | A B C D | 11 | A B C D | 21 | A B C D | 31 | A B C D |
| 2 | A B C D | 12 | A B C D | 22 | A B C D | 32 | A B C D |
| 3 | A B C D | 13 | A B C D | 23 | A B C D | 33 | A B C D |
| 4 | A B C D | 14 | A B C D | 24 | A B C D | 34 | A B C D |
| 5 | A B C D | 15 | A B C D | 25 | A B C D | 35 | A B C D |
| 6 | A B C D | 16 | A B C D | 26 | A B C D | 36 | A B C D |
| 7 | A B C D | 17 | A B C D | 27 | A B C D | 37 | A B C D |
| 8 | A B C D | 18 | A B C D | 28 | A B C D | 38 | A B C D |
| 9 | A B C D | 19 | A B C D | 29 | A B C D | 39 | A B C D |
| 10 | A B C D | 20 | A B C D | 30 | A B C D | 40 | A B C D |

FCE/CPE-1 SUP    KENRICK & JEFFERSON    Printers to the Computer Industry    DP135 11

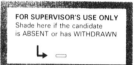

UNIVERSITY OF CAMBRIDGE
LOCAL EXAMINATIONS SYNDICATE
INTERNATIONAL EXAMINATIONS

# ENGLISH AS A FOREIGN LANGUAGE

Examination/Paper No.

Examination Title

Centre/Candidate No.

Candidate Name

● Sign here if the information above is correct.

● Tell the Invigilator immediately if the
  information above is not correct.

## LISTENING COMPREHENSION ANSWER SHEET

ENTER TEST
NUMBER HERE →

FOR OFFICE
USE ONLY →    [10][20][30][40][50]
              [1][2][3][4][5][6][7][8][9]

| # | | # | | # | |
|---|---|---|---|---|---|
| 1 | | 1 | 21 | 21 | |
| 2 | | 2 | 22 | 22 | |
| 3 | | 3 | 23 | 23 | |
| 4 | | 4 | 24 | 24 | |
| 5 | | 5 | 25 | 25 | |
| 6 | | 6 | 26 | 26 | |
| 7 | | 7 | 27 | 27 | |
| 8 | | 8 | 28 | 28 | |
| 9 | | 9 | 29 | 29 | |
| 10 | | 10 | 30 | 30 | |
| 11 | | 11 | 31 | 31 | |
| 12 | | 12 | 32 | 32 | |
| 13 | | 13 | 33 | 33 | |
| 14 | | 14 | 34 | 34 | |
| 15 | | 15 | 35 | 35 | |
| 16 | | 16 | 36 | 36 | |
| 17 | | 17 | 37 | 37 | |
| 18 | | 18 | 38 | 38 | |
| 19 | | 19 | 39 | 39 | |
| 20 | | 20 | 40 | 40 | |

EFL-4    KENRICK■JEFFERSON    Printers to the Computer Industry    DP150/31